the Eucharist

the Eucharist:
the Bread of Life

ERNEST LUSSIER S.S.S.

ALBA · HOUSE   NEW · YORK

SOCIETY OF ST. PAUL, 2187 VICTORY BLVD., STATEN ISLAND, NEW YORK 10314

Library of Congress Cataloging in Publication Data

Lussier, Ernest, 1911-
   The Eucharist : the bread of life.

   Bibliography: p.
   1. Lord's Supper--Catholic Church. I. Title.
BX2215.2.L85   234'.163   77-3035
ISBN 0-8189-0349-X

Imprimi Potest
Normand Falardeau, S.S.S.
Provincial

Nihil Obstat:
James T. O'Connor, S.T.D.
Censor Librorum

Imprimatur:
+*James P. Mahoney, D.D.*
Vicar General, Archdiocese of New York
March 9, 1977

The Nihil Obstat and Imprimatur
are a declaration that a book or pamphlet is considered
to be free from doctrinal or moral error. It is not implied that
those who have granted the Nihil Obstat and Imprimatur agree
with the contents, opinions or statements expressed.

Designed, printed and bound in the United States of
America by the Fathers and Brothers of the Society of St. Paul,
2187 Victory Boulevard, Staten Island, New York, 10314,
as part of their communications apostolate.

1 2 3 4 5 6 7 8 9 (Current Printing: first digit).

DEDICATION

TO MY NEPHEWS AND NIECES

ANNETTE LUSSIER AND AUGUSTINO GAGLIARDI
AND THEIR CHILDREN
MARIE ANNETTE, CHRISTINA,
AUGUSTINO, NICHOLAS,
AND ELISE

AUTHOR'S PREFACE

This volume completes the trilogy begun with **Getting To Know The Eucharist** (Alba House 1974) and **Living The Eucharistic Mystery** (Alba House 1976). Here again the approach to the Eucharist is by way of meditative reflection based on the "warm and living love for Scripture to which," according to Vatican II, "the venerable tradition of both Eastern and Western rites gives testimony" (SC 24). Besides the learned approach of scholars, there is also the area of meditative contemplation of the Eucharistic mystery which is perhaps too easily bypassed, yet is surely most fruitful and productive for Christian living.

This book might help to extend the good influence of the recent International Eucharistic Congress held in Philadelphia August 1-8, 1976. This meeting has evidently been a great success: "It may be that this Congress has been the most important event for American Catholics since Vatican II," **Commonweal**, August 27, 1976, p. 551. See also **America**, August 21, 1976, pp. 73-75. It is now up to us to strive to penetrate more deeply and to live more fully, the many splendors of the Eucharistic mystery.

Ernest Lussier, SSS

CONTENTS

A. THE EUCHARIST: The Bread of Life

The notions of symbol and sign are basic for the intelligence of the sacraments. The sacraments are signs of faith; they are an essential part of our spiritual life. Sacramental theology must see the sacraments in relation to Christ, to the Holy Spirit, and to the Church. The sacraments are our means of entering the mystery of Christ and of his Church, our way of living in a full personal community setting.

Hunger and bread are frequently recurring Biblical themes. The people complain for food in the wilderness (Ex 16:2-3, Nb 11:4-6). Dt 8:2-3 moralizes on this situation. Mk 2:23-28 tells about the Apostles plucking corn on the Sabbath. Our Lord was hungry after his fast (Mt. 4:3-4). The cause of hunger is sometimes persecution (Jr 38:9) or sloth (Pr 19:15); more often hunger is presented as a divine punishment (Jr 11:22). Hunger has dire effects (Is 8:21, Pr 6:30, 1 Cor 4:11). The charity of men should provide relief from hunger (Pr 25:21, Mt 25:35-44). Spiritual hunger receives special attention (Am 8:11-12). Our Lord proclaims a beatitude for the hungry (Mt 5:6, Lk 6:2, 25). He himself is the bread of life (Jn 6:35, 51-58).

Water and thirst are important biblical themes. The Mosaic water miracle (Ex 17:3-7, Nb 20:11) is often referred to in various Biblical passages, Deuteronomist (Dt 28:48) and prophetic (Is 41:17-18, Ezk 47:1-12). The sapiential writers also use the theme of water (Pr 13:14, Si 24:23-29, Pr 25:21-22). Jesus also mentions water or thirst to inculcate moral lessons (Mt 10:42, 25:31-46). He experienced thirst (Jn 4:6-7, Mk 15:23, Jn 19:28-30). Following the example of the Old Testament writers, Jesus also used the words thirst and water figuratively (Is 55:1, Mt 5:6, Jn 4:13-14, 7:37-39). The Christian must also drink Christ's blood (Jn 6:53-56).

Taking a meal together has always been a sign of friendship and hospitality, of human solidarity and of communion with the deity. Significant celebrations of human life and important interventions of God in salvation history include a meal: birth of Isaac (Gn 18:1-15), manna (Ex 16), ratification of treaties (Gn 31:54, Ex 18:12), covenant on Sinai (Ex 24:10-11), the Passover meal (Ex 12, Jn 1:29, 1 Cor 5:7-8, Jn 19:36), the communion sacrifice (Lv 3), the Messianic banquet (Is 25:6).

Meals played an important role in the life and teaching of our Lord. His meals with sinners manifested the new era of forgiveness which he was inaugurating. The miracle of the loaves is a Messianic sign, an anticipation of the Messianic banquet of the time of fulfillment. The meals of Jesus with his disciples were a sign of his sharing with them of his mission (Mk 10:38-39, Col 1:24). The final stage of salvation is presented as the eschato-

logical banquet (Mt 8:11, 22:1-14). It is in the context of
these Biblical meals that is found the meaning of the
Last Supper.

1 Cor 11:17-34 gives directions for the proper celebration of the Lord's Supper at Corinth, in view of correcting
some prevalent disorders. This passage is especially important for it contains not only the oldest account of the
institution of the Lord's Supper, written as much as ten
years before Mark's, but also Paul's understanding of its
significance.

St. Paul regards the Eucharist as a means of communion with Christ (1 Cor 10:16-17), as a sign of brotherhood by which all Christians are united together (1 Cor
10:17), as a memorial of Christ and of his death for man
(1 Cor 11:24-26). He records Christ's words which describe the Eucharist as the seal of the New Covenant
(1 Cor 11:25). Paul's language is markedly realistic. Ph
3:10-14 is a good description provided by St. Paul of the
right dispositions required for the reception of the Eucharist. St. Luke's account (22:14-20) resembles most the
liturgical tradition reproduced by St. Paul in 1 Cor 11:
23-25.

For Mark the Lord's Supper is at once a bond of union
with Christ, a covenant, a sacrifice (14:24), and an anticipation of the eschatological Messianic feast (25). Mt 26:
26-29 follows Mark's text closely with a few additions.
Finally, the chapter underlines the theological and apologetic importance of the Last Supper.

The sacraments of Baptism and of the Eucharist play an important role in St. John's Gospel. The conversation with Nicodemus (Jn 3:1-21) refers to Baptism. The discourse on the bread of life ultimately deals with the Eucharist (Jn 6:51-58). The miracles of Cana (2:1-11) and of the multiplication of the loaves (6:1-15) include some Eucharistic symbolism. Baptism and the Eucharist are suggested in 19:34. Why St. John does not mention the institution of the Eucharist.

These words take on particular meaning according to who pronounces them: Jesus at the Last Supper, the priest at the altar, and every believer at the crossroads of his life. Christ really gives himself to us personally in the Eucharist to be our bread of life. The custom of visualizing the Eucharist by solemn exposition has surely much good traditional thinking in its favor. The reception of holy Communion and prayer before the Blessed Sacrament both have the same object and purpose.

In the Eucharist Christian ethics, that is, moral action, motivation, and character find their source and their purpose. For Jesus to eat and to drink is to do God's will in total self-offering to God. The Christian must do the same after the example of his Lord, by total commitment to Christ and to his principles. A Christian lets himself be eaten by making himself available for the service of all men.

The presence of God's grace in our heart is the purpose of all Christ's presences in our life, and most especially of his Eucharistic presence. Two presences of Christ stand out as exceptional because of their essentially objective nature, above all the Eucharistic presence, but also Christ's presence in Scripture as its ultimate contents, the Word of God's inspired revelation. And both of these presences are conveniently united in the Eucharistic celebration.

In the Old Testament the ends of sacrifice in relation to God were adoration, thanksgiving, expiation, and petition. All the life of Jesus was a sacrifice, but his death was the climax of his self-dedication to God, and his resurrection was God's acceptance of the sacrifice. For us Christians also, all our life is a sacrifice, with and in Christ's sacrifice (1 P 2:4-5, Rm 12:1). The Eucharist for Christ is a clear statement of purpose and a legacy. For us it is the source and origin of our Christian life.

The union of the faithful with Christ is realized in the highest degree in the Eucharist (1 Cor 10:16). Christian fellowship or communion is sharing a common life in Christ through the Holy Spirit. Communion with Christ gives us a share in material but especially in spiritual realities and above all in God's own life. Our Christian life in Christ unites us with the Father and his Son in the Holy Spirit. St. Paul views our communion with God as our adoption as children of God.

St. John explains the inwardness of the Christian's
spiritual life as a divine-human fellowship or communion.
He describes our Christian life of union with God in different ways. By it a Christian lives in God and God lives
in him; he is begotten by God, has new life from him;
he is from God, God's child. In 1 Jn to know God is a highlight in our communion with God. Faith and love are
visible evidence of true union with God who is light
(1 Jn 1:5) and love (4:8, 16).

The holy Eucharist is the means of integrating our
own personal spiritual history into God's total redeeming plan. Christ gave us this sacrament as the spiritual
food of our soul by which we are nourished and fortified
by living his very life. The Eucharist is the antidote
which frees us from our daily faults and preserves us
from mortal sin. It is the symbol of the one body whose
head is Christ and to which Christ wants us as members
to be closely united by faith, hope, and love. The Eucharist is our daily bread, offering us the grace we need to
carry our cross daily. Our daily life should be the continuation of our communion and the preparation for the
one to follow.

There is something new about Christian Eucharistic
worship that sets it apart from all other religions, even
from the revealed religion of the Old Testament. The
originality of the New Testament worship is its intimate
relation to our Christian life. The Eucharist is the new
covenant predicted by Jeremiah (31:31-34) and Ezechiel

(36:26-27) and characterized by the interiorization of religion.

This essential aspect of the renewal of God's covenant with man is underlined by St. John in 6:29, 32-33, 45 and in chapter 13 where the establishment of the new covenant is practically identified with the gift of the new commandment. There is an indissoluble link between the gift of the Spirit and of the Eucharist, the gift of love, love of Christ for us and the love we owe our neighbor.

Luke in Acts (2:42-47, 4:32-35) gives the ideal facets of the first Christian community; fidelity to the teaching of the Apostles, to fraternal communion, to the breaking of the bread, and to the prayers. The breaking of the bread, the celebration of the Eucharist, is intimately related to the teaching of the Apostles and to fraternal communion. This Christian fellowship consists essentially in inner unity, in being of one heart and soul (Ac 4:32); it is a condition of Christian worship and also its principal effect.

Israel in its sacred history expressed its special relation with God by the idea of covenant. A series of covenants make up our biblical salvation history, especially five: the covenants with Adam, Noah, Abraham, and Moses, and finally the new and everlasting covenant with, through, and in Christ. Jesus himself is God's covenant with man which finds its full actuation in the holy Eucharist.

Both liturgical and personal worship need the balance of adoration, thanksgiving, confession, and petition that comes from hearing and meditating on God's word, and both require that dedication of commitment to discipleship congruent with being members one of another in the one Body of Christ. There is a marvelous unity in the essence of prayer, as much as in its different forms. The Bible is the source of this unity and its focus is on Christ. Ultimately all Christian prayer is centered on the prayer of Christ himself (Heb 7:25).

Theologians today feel the need of insisting on the spiritual theology of the sacraments and their ethical context. For the Eucharist this means insistence on the meal character of the sacrament and its influence in the Christian life. The notions of personal liberty and conscience, the theology of the word, of liberation, of symbolism all have important contributions to make to modern Eucharistic theology. The same is true for the basic ideas of truth, beauty, goodness, and unity.

B. Historical and Theological Notes

A brief history of the Cenacle: description of actual traditional site and survey of its historical and archeological background; important text of St. Epiphanius; the great basilica named "Holy Sion"; Franciscan custody; Cenacle today; modern Church of the Dormition.

The excavation of the catacombs at Rome was the work of the fossores or diggers. In the third century they were counted among the clergy at the lowest grade. Pope Damasus is renowned for his magnificent inscriptions in honor of the martyrs. He placed one of his famous inscriptions on the tomb of St. Tarcisius in the catacombs of Callistus.

Eucharistic gatherings in the catacombs were more the exception than the rule. The Eucharist, however, was apparently offered there at first as part of the refrigerium for the dead and later in honor of the martyrs.

The fish as a hieroglyph for Christ was susceptible of varied application and remained a favorite theme of early Christian iconography. It was used in a special sense for Christ as food and thus for the Eucharist, witness the inscriptions of Abercius (the oldest stone monument mentioning the Eucharist) and of Pectorius.

A catacombal painting symbolizing the Eucharist is found in the crypt of Lucina and dates back to the middle of the second century. The oldest known representation of the Eucharist is a fresco in the cemetery of Priscilla. Another representation (beginning of third century) is found in the cemetery of Callistus. The idea of the celestial banquet appears in later catacombal art. The themes of the Good Shepherd and of the Orant are also significant.

There are several reasons to justify calling St. Thomas
Aquinas, the Doctor of the Eucharist. He is prominent
in Raphael's great fresco, the Disputa. His authorship of
the liturgical texts for the feast of Corpus Christi, however, is not as extensive as has been supposed.

The teaching of our post-Vatican II Church as found
in the official texts. The phenomenon of Ecumenical
Agreed Statements. Reactions to the Encyclical MF. Remarks on the Instruction EM and on the preface to the
new Sacramentary. Four subjects that will be treated in
the next chapter. Three main directions taken by current
Eucharistic theology in its process of renewal.

Considers four important points of Eucharistic theology: transubstantiation; Christ's presence in the Eucharist as a personal presence; the central nature of the
Eucharistic celebration as the Paschal Mystery; the social, communitarian nature of Christian worship and the
ethical approach to the sacrament. Also some remarks
on Eucharistic devotions and a short bibliography on the
new theology of the Eucharist.

List of Abbreviations

AG—Ad Gentes
Decree on the Church's Missionary Activity

DENZ.-SCHON.—Enchiridion Symbolorum

EM—Eucharisticum Mysterium
Instruction on the Worship of the Eucharistic Mystery

ES—Eucharistiae Sacramentum
Instruction on Holy Communion and the Worship of the Eucharistic Mystery outside of Mass

GS—Gaudium et Spes
Constitution on the Church in the Modern World

LG—Lumen Gentium
Dogmatic Constitution on the Church

MF—Mysterium Fidei
Encyclical on Eucharistic Doctrine and Worship

PO—Presbyterorum Ordinis
Decree on the Ministry and Life of Priests

SC—Sacrosanctum Concilium
Constitution on the Sacred Liturgy

UR—Unitatis Redintegratio
Decree on Ecumenism

INTRODUCTION

The Church continually seeks to have the faithful understand and live the Eucharist more fully. It is through the Eucharist that the faithful come to express in their lives and to manifest to others the mystery of Christ and the true nature of the Church.

With this volume, Father Lussier completes a trilogy on the great Mystery of Faith. He has endeavored to help his readers **to know, to live** and **to meditate** on the many splendored mystery of the Eucharist. The riches of this mystery cannot be fully or adequately expressed in any series of books. Yet, Father Lussier presents us with a series of doctrinal meditations, designed to arouse sentiments of ardent love and fervent devotion, similar to those which the author himself reflects so eloquently in his writings.

The meditations are intended to activate a loving concern for the spiritual and material needs of others, just as the Eucharist is God's great gift of His love and concern for us. The latter section of the book contains interesting historical and theological notes, including present trends in Eucharistic theology. These trends show how theologians—faithful to the teachings of the Church—strive to deepen our understanding of the mystery of the Eucharist.

For some the notion of mystery is incompatible with their assumption that the powers of human comprehension are unlimited. But the Eucharist is an overwhelming mystery. How and why is it that Jesus, the Son of God, who came to this world in human flesh, now remains with us under the appearance of bread and wine? Why is God so good to us? Our belief and our witness to the life and love of our Eucharistic Lord may spur others to investigate God's goodness to us.

The first two books of the trilogy served as a remote and a proximate preparation for the 41st International Eucharistic Congress. At the Congress in Philadelphia, Cardinals, Archbishops, Bishops, priests, religious and lay persons from every state of the union and from many foreign lands gave magnificent witness to their faith in, and devotion to, Jesus in the Eucharist, and of their solidarity with one another because of that belief. The various special celebrations by peoples of varying racial or ethnic heritage and different age groups gave witness to the reality that the center point of the different celebrations was ever the same—the sacrifice of the Mass by which Our Eucharistic Lord is made present among us.

The theme of the Congress—The Eucharist and the Hungers of the Human Family—and the various programs and conferences highlighted the truth that the Eucharistic Sacrifice is the source and summit of the Christian life—which essentially is a Eucharistic life. Our faith in the Eucharist cannot be sterile. It must be fruitful. The Eucharist must be lived. It must be reflected in our lives.

Father Lussier presents this final volume of the trilogy with the wish that it might "help to extend the good influence of the Congress." It cannot help but do that, motivated as it is by his own deep understanding and his ardent love for Jesus the Bread of Life.

John Cardinal Krol
Archbishop of Philadelphia

October 1, 1976.

the Eucharist

A. THE EUCHARIST: The Bread of Life

1.

THE SACRAMENTS

Theologians today are paying particular attention to sacramentality. We find a proliferation of articles and books on this subject, a clear indication of the thinking and problems of our day. The reasons for this special interest are many: first the return to the sources method of research, but also renewed interest in spirituality with clearer focusing on the supernatural, and especially the mystery of the Incarnation, and that of the Church and of the holy Eucharist. Dom Casel's theology of the mysteries is perhaps the most fruitful theological idea of our century because of the light it sheds on the nature of the Eucharistic sacrifice. It is also an excellent reaction and catalyst for the climate of dechristianization and secularization which afflicts people today, when some are even asking whether there is a future to the sacraments, as if they can hardly be salvaged in our modern civilization. The sacraments, however, will always be the heart of our worship and spiritual living.

The word sacrament is closely related to the Greek mystery. According to its etymology and in reality the sacrament is something beyond the capacity of our human comprehension. The notions of symbol and sign remain basic for the intelligence of the sacrament, notions that are very popular today in the natural sciences (psychology, linguistics, semiology). To communicate with one another and to react to our vital environment man cannot do without signs and symbols. Our sacramental signs, we are told by some, no longer mean anything to our generation, which is characterized by ceaseless and constant evolution. Yet our sacramental symbols are among the simplest and closest to nature (water, oil, bread and wine) and are easily accessible to men at all times. There is no reason why we should abandon these primitive agrarian human symbols in favor, for example, of others referring to our industrial and technical civilization, for example, an oil change, a check up, a purgative, a transfusion, intravenous feeding. In any case our sacraments are essentially related to the history of our salvation in Christ. They are given to us by God and our essential reaction is to receive them humbly in faith. Adaptation is possible only in continuity with our traditional past and the limits of our faith. And to those who would insist that our faith and our hope mean little for our contemporaries it should be pointed out that no one can be dispensed from initiation to the mystery of salvation as contained in divine revelation, especially the New Testament which is unique and never will be repeated. Adaptation is necessary, but man also must make the necessary effort, today as always, to come, meet, and accept God in Christ.

Formerly sacramental theology stressed the matter and form of the sacraments thus underlining their minimal essentials and their efficacy considered as causality. The sacramental symbolism was easily relegated to the background. The stress on their validity obscured somewhat their reality. Today the liturgy stresses the ritual context, and the mystery depth of the sacraments, as also their biblical background; all of these considerations are not always an absolute condition for the sacrament's efficacy, but have nonetheless their importance in the organic whole of the sacrament.

The key problem of the pastoral approach to the sacraments is probably no longer validity and liceity, but **faith** and sacrament as spiritual mystery. And these are not two parallel ways of going to God, independent of each other.

The sacraments are sacraments of faith. The validity **(opus operatum)** of the sacrament is not linked to the faith of the minister, but it is based on the faith of the Church. And the faith of the recipient conditions the sacrament's efficacy which is proportionate to the fervor of the one receiving (baptism of infants is exceptional and based on the faith of the parents and of the Church).

Faith disposes one for the sacrament. The sacrament in turn expresses our faith. It is a profession of faith, an action which manifests better than mere words, the realities of faith; it animates, stimulates, fortifies our faith. The sacraments confer supernatural life, and give us a participation in the realities of faith. The sacramental liturgy is the means of establishing the communion of the faithful with God and of inserting him in the mystery of Christ. "The sacraments not only presuppose faith, but by words and objects they also nourish, strengthen and express it; that is why they are called sacraments of faith. They do indeed impart grace, but in addition, the very act of celebrating them disposes the faithful most effectively to receive this grace in a fruitful manner, to worship God duly and to practice charity" (SC, no. 59).

The question has practical consequences. For example evangelization and sacramentalization must go hand in hand. Granted that a man must be humanized, before he is Christianized and sacramentalized, yet these activities are not juxtaposed but interact one on the other and are not separate levels of operation. To do otherwise would be divisive of the mission of the Church and to do violence to divine revelation. Our works of beneficence must be motivated by Christian principles and lead ultimately to the love and worship of God.

Sacrament does rhyme with medicament but sacraments are much more than a remedy for sin which is a negative result. They are an essential part of our spiritual life. They are not isolated acts but really form an organism with the Eucharist as their center and focal point. They introduce us into the mystery of the divine life, by modeling us mystically after the death and resurrection of Christ. They re-enact for us the Paschal event and realize the paradox of eternity in our time, by anticipating for us the eschatological kingdom. By them all our human life acquires a cultural and sacrificial dimension, in Christ and in the Church. Our Christian life is essentially a mystical life and only secondarily a moral life. Morality is the logical consequence of our insertion in the Christian mystery.

Those who look down on the sacraments, evidently have no use for the sacramentals, those pious customs born of the secular, age-old piety of the Church, such as the sign of the cross, the use of holy water, genuflexion, blessings even with the Blessed Sacrament. This again is to be deplored and is surely not according to the mind of Vatican II which states clearly that popular devotions are warmly recommended provided they are harmonized with the liturgy and are derived from it and lead people to it (SC, no. 13).

Sacramental theology must see the sacraments in relation to Christ, to the Holy Spirit, and to the Church.

Christ is the author of the sacraments and the principal agent in their celebration. They are a prolongation of the Incarnation and the reactualization of the mysteries of our redemption, Christ's personal, effective, and sovereign action being the source of the gift of all sacramental grace. They are a continuation and a supplement for the presence of the Incarnate Christ, the embodiment

of the actual saving action of our risen Lord. Christ himself is the sacrament of our encounter with God, in a
transcendent sense of the word sacrament, in an eminent
way; the seven sacraments are our God-given means of
assimilating the mystery of our salvation through Christ
and in Christ.

The sacraments are also the work of the Holy Spirit;
it is by the sacraments that the original Pentecost is
always operative in the Church. By appropriation all
work of sanctification is attributed to the Holy Spirit and
it is clear that all the sacraments introduce us into the
mystery of the supernatural life. It is the Holy Spirit
who works and guarantees the efficacy of the sacramental
rites; "May all of us who share in the body and blood of
Christ, be brought together in unity by the Holy Spirit"
(Eucharistic Prayer II). "By your Holy Spirit gather all
who share this bread and wine into the one body of
Christ" (Eucharistic Prayer IV). There is also a close
relation between sacrament and prayer and worship;
now Christian prayer and worship are the special pre-
serve of the Holy Spirit. "He makes us cry out, Abba,
Father" (Rm 8:15). "Those who worship must worship
in spirit and in truth" (Jn 4:24). Finally, the Holy Spirit
himself is the fruit of our reception of the sacraments.
"Grant that we, who are nourished by his body and
blood, may be filled with his Holy Spirit and become one
body, one Spirit in Christ" (Eucharistic Prayer III).

The role of the Church in the sacraments is of the
greatest significance. A constant theme in Vatican II is
the presentation of the Church, like Christ himself, as
a sacrament, a visible sign and an efficacious means, at
the service of all mankind. The sacrament of salvation,
of unity for the human race, of our sharing of the very
life of God (LG, nos. 1, 9), the Church is the sacrament
of our encounter with Christ, as he is the sacrament of
our encounter with God, and in the same transcendent

sense. Like Christ, with him, through him, and in him the Church is the basic sacrament of salvation receiving from him the seven sacraments and administering them to God's people. This theology is an excellent presentation of the unity of the ecclesial reality under its double aspect of visibility and invisibility, structure and happening. The Church is a complex entity forming "one interlocked reality which is comprised of a human and a divine element. For this reason, by an excellent analogy, this reality is compared to the mystery of the Incarnate Word" (LG, no. 8).

The sacraments along with the faith of God's people are the heart of the Church. They are the actions, the gestes of the Church as well as of Christ. Their administration, or better their celebration belong to the Church. They are always and everywhere given in the name of the Church, or better still in the person of the Church. The Church alone has power and right over the sacraments; the minister can only act as the Church's delegate and according to the Church's intention; the Church, however, understood in its total reality which includes all its members, each one participating actively according to his proper rank and condition in the whole assembly of the faithful.

Our holy mother, the Church, is a traditional expression of tenderness and respect which describes well the fruitfulness of the Church as an instrument of salvation, especially in the celebration of the sacraments, the fountains of grace. This is the celebration of the whole Church, the people of God gathered around their priests and sharing in their priesthood, the official worship of the Church. With due respect for the special sacrament of Holy Orders, the true minister of the sacraments is the loving Church, the whole Christian community, the mother with her children. That is why the sacrament depends not on the virtue of the presiding minister, on

his faith and charity but on the faith and sanctity of the
Church itself. According to St. Albert the Great, "the
nest of the Church is formed by the sacraments." Viewed
in an ecumenical spirit the saying would see in the true
sacraments found among our separated brethren, a ves-
tige, a beginning of our hoped for unity, the return of
all God's children to the unity of Christ's Church: "How
often have I longed to gather your children, as a hen
gathers her chicks under her wings, and you refused"
(Mt 23:37).

The intention of doing what the Church does is absolutely necessary for the validity of the sacrament; this
shows the essential relation of the sacrament to the
Church. On this score the juridical context of matter and
form has perhaps been overstressed to the detriment of
the vital context necessary for the full fruitfulness of
the sacraments, for example, the performance of a fervent liturgy and especially the participation of the faithful in the celebration. The social character is inherent to
any act of worship. Since it is the whole Church that
celebrates the sacraments, it is also the Church that gives
the true meaning to the actions of the sacramental ministers.

There is the consequent question of another relation
between the Church and the sacraments, the power the
Church exercises over the sacraments. These are primarily the actions of Christ, but also if secondarily and
dependent on Christ, the actions of the Church, her
dowry as some of the Fathers have stated. The sacraments are evidently intended by Christ for the use of his
Church and are directly under her authority and juris-
diction. The principle is clearly stated already at the
Council of Trent. The Church, respecting the essence of
the sacraments, that is, their essential relation to Christ,
has considerable power in their administration. "The
Church may decree or change what will promote the

usefulness of the sacraments or underline the respect
that is their due, according to what it judges more appropriate to the circumstances of time and place" **(Denz.
Schon.** 1728).

The liturgical renewal has focused much attention on
the participation of the community in the celebration of
the sacraments. Thus, for example, the anointing of the
sick is often rightly presented as the assembly of the
Church in prayer with the suffering Christian. Well and
good, provided the essential dimension of the efficacy of
the sacrament is given the privileged consideration it
deserves.

There is today a proper reaction to the exclusively
individualistic conception of the grace of the sacraments,
to an egoistic and strictly private approach to God. Even
St. Thomas' distinction could be misleading when he
states that two sacraments, Holy Orders and Matrimony,
are necessary for the Church considered as a community
and represent social values, whereas the other five are
ordained to the good of the individual (III q. 65, art. 1
and 2).

Actually all the sacraments are for the service of the
Church and build up the body of Christ. They are remedies for sin and helps for personal sanctification but also
and essentially means of mystical incorporation in Christ.
Baptism and Confirmation serve for basic incorporation;
penance repairs or renews our union with God in the
Church; the Eucharist in a special way seals and develops
ecclesial communion. The social implications of Marriage
and Holy Orders are quite clear, and the anointing of the
sick preserves them for the community either by restor-
ing their health or by giving them the courage to endure
their sufferings.

The salvation that God offers us in Christ is eminently
social, ecclesial. It is found only in the unity of the mystical body which is the Church. Grace is obtained only in

the measure of our vital union with Christ's Church. And this union is effected by the sacraments which are not only Christian passwords or rallying banners, but especially actions which incorporate us into the Church, the center of our life for God in Christ and his Holy Spirit.

According to St. Ambrose we are redeemed by the grace of the Church. Theologians today say practically the same when they like to see the Church as the intermediate effect of the sacraments **(res et sacramentum)** namely the sign and cause of the grace of the sacraments. The same is said of Christ, especially in the Eucharist which is the focal point of all the sacraments.

Briefly, the sacraments are our means of entering the mystery of Christ and of his Church, our way of living in a full personal and community setting. Two attitudes manifested by our contemporaries are equally baffling. Some are deserting sacramental practice because of their disaffection for institutional ritual, yet remain united in fervent small community groups. For others the sacraments have absolute quasi-divine beauty but a dragon Church is in charge of these treasures. In both instances we have a far cry from Augustinian thought: **"O Sancta Mater Ecclesia, veritatem sola tu habes et in lacte tuo et in pane tuo."**

2.

HUNGER AND BREAD

Hunger, the need for food, and bread, the most common staple in the human diet, are frequently recurring Biblical themes.

In the wilderness the Hebrews complained that they were led out of Egypt where food was plentiful and they taunted Moses for wanting to have them die of famine. It was then that God sent the quails and the manna. "The whole community of the sons of Israel began to complain against Moses and Aaron in the wilderness and said to them, Why did we not die at Yahweh's hand in the land of Egypt, where we were able to sit down to pans of meat and could eat bread to our heart's content? As it is, you have brought us to this wilderness to starve this whole community to death" (Ex 16:2-3). The murmuring in the wilderness is a constant motif of the desert wandering. The people preferred the seasoned foods of the flesh-pots of Egypt to the precarious freedom of the wilderness. The Sinai peninsula is barren, and the Israelites could not have subsisted on what they might have foraged. Yet all that had been hard in Egypt is forgotten now, and they idealize the past. The people now prefer food to liberty, and even to life itself.

"The sons of Israel began to wail again, Who will give us meat to eat? Think of the fish we used to eat free in Egypt, the cucumbers, melons, leeks, onions, and garlic. Here we are wasting away stripped of everything; there is nothing but manna for us to look at" (Nb 11:4-6). Not satisfied with the manna, the people craved seasoned meat dishes such as they had enjoyed in Egypt. The mention of plenty of food in Egypt is a regular feature of their behavior when things went wrong, even though the food there consisted mainly of fish and vegetables. Yet if manna tasted like butter-cakes kneaded with olive oil, it is not surprising that the Israelites longed for a change of diet to include the sharp tang of onions and garlic.

Deuteronomy moralizes on the miraculous food given by God in the wilderness. "Remember how Yahweh your God led you in the wilderness to humble you, to test you, and know your inmost heart, whether you would keep his commandments or not. He humbled you, he made you feel hunger, he fed you with manna which neither you nor your fathers had known, to make you understand that man does not live on bread alone but that man lives on everything that comes from the mouth of God" (Dt 8:2-3). Spiritual as well as physical forces sustain human existence, as was recognized by Christ at his temptation (Mt 4:4). To deny the existence and reality of spiritual factors is to separate oneself from a fundamentally important area of reality. Bread is a necessity for physical existence but the basis of a human society collapses where it is solely economic. The higher life is not only the true life of man but it is even a necessity for his economic life. And when all is said and done, a man's real life does not depend on the satisfaction of physical hunger. Even basic physical necessities are subordinate to the revealed word of God. The word of God is more vital to man's existence than the food he eats.

One day the apostles were hungry on the Sabbath and ate heads of grain from the fields they were crossing, plucking some of the heads and eating them after rubbing them in their hands (Lk 6:1) to separate the grain from the husks. The Pharisees object not to their picking of the grain for that was allowable (Dt 23:36) but for

doing so on the Sabbath. Our Lord vindicates them (Mk
2:25-26) by referring back to the incident when David
and his men ate the bread which was reserved for the
priests (1 S 21:2-7). David was excused from the law,
as any man would have been, by the circumstances of
his extreme hunger. The claims of human needs have
greater authority than ritual regulations. The Pharisees
care about the legal point, Jesus about the human need.
Both in the case of David and of his disciples, the higher
law was that of man's necessary bodily needs.

Our Lord was hungry after fasting for forty days in
the wilderness of Juda, thus showing his perfect humanity (Mt 4:3). His first temptation is to interpret the assurance of divine sonship in a selfish and materialistic way.
Its form is interesting in view of the feeding of the multitude later on; that miracle is not a selfish or arbitrary
exercise of power, but an expression of concern for
human needs and a prophetic sign of Christ's gift to men
of the true spiritual bread. The three temptations can be
summed up as temptations to use extraordinary Messianic power. The first temptation is to use miraculous
power to provide for ordinary material needs. The Roman
rulers found very soon that one way to gain favor of the
masses was to distribute free bread. Jesus' task, however,
is to declare God's message, not to fill stomachs, although
on occasion he does that also. A man's real life does not
depend on the satisfaction of physical hunger. Hence our
Lord's apt quote of Dt 8:3.

Again Jesus is hungry, when on Monday of holy week,
he looks for figs on a barren fig tree. Not finding any fruit
in spite of a luxuriant foliage, Jesus expresses his dis-
appointment by cursing the tree which withers and dies
(Mt 21:18-19). This is a symbolic action in which the fig
tree represents Israel who will be punished for its fruit-
lessness, the lack of the faith which God had a right to
expect.

Revelation (7:16) describes the reward of the saints
in heaven as the absence of any unfulfilled desires. "They
will never hunger or thirst again, because the Lamb who
is at the throne will be their shepherd." We will be happy
in our freedom from the inconveniences of this present
life, want and pain. Christ assuages the hunger and thirst
of man by providing in himself the antidote of our rest-
lessness, the complete counterpart of our unsatisfied
desires.

Sometimes the **cause** of hunger is persecution. Jeremiah (38:9) was thrown into a miry cistern that he might
die of hunger and starvation in the mud. He was rescued
through the kindness of an Ethiopian servant of the court.
Sloth can also be the cause of hunger. "An idle person
will suffer hunger" (Pr 19:15). Because of his inactivity
the feckless, the sluggard has no means of satisfying his
hunger. More often according to the Old Testament idea
of earthly retribution, hunger is presented as the effect
of God's justice punishing the wicked (Jr 11:22). Am 4:6
has a striking figure of speech for famine; it is cleanness
of teeth through lack of food.

Hunger has dire **effects.** It leads one to murmur
against God (Is 8:21); it inclines one to robbery (Pr 6:30);
it serves as an image for frustration (Is 29:8). St. Paul,
however, does not view it as an obstacle in the service of
God; in fact, it seems to be something that the missioner
should expect (1 Cor 4:11). For Paul nothing can touch
the one thing that really matters, that is, God's loving
care for the younger brothers and sisters of his Son, and
the corresponding answer of our love for God. "Nothing
can come between us and the love of Christ, even if we
are troubled or worried, or being persecuted, or lacking
food or clothes" (Rm 8:35). None of the dangers and
troubles of life can make the true Christian forget the
love of Christ made known to men in his death and resurrection. God's love will never let go of his own whatever

strains and pressures are brought to bear on them. There
is no factor or force in the universe that is not under the
control of God who made it, and he is for us. These things
might tempt the believer to think that his Lord has for-
saken him. St. Paul assures us that this cannot be really
so; the separation is but seeming.

The charity of men should provide **relief** for the
hunger, of their fellow men. "Share your bread with the
hungry" (Is 58:7). "The upright man gives his own bread
to the hungry" (Ezk 18:7). It is wrong to refuse bread to
the famished (Jb 22:7). We must give food even to our
enemies (Pr 25:21). Our Lord considers done to himself
the charity exercised toward those who are hungry. "I
was hungry and you gave me food . . . Lord, when did
we see you hungry and feed you? . . . Truly, I say to you,
as you did it to one of the least of these my brethren, you
did it to me . . . I was hungry and you gave me no food . . .
Lord, when did we see you hungry and did not minister
to you? . . . Truly, as you did it not to one of the least of
these, you did it not to me . . ." (Mt 25:35-44). Jesus not
only singles out the poor and the wretched as objects of
special solicitude, he identifies himself with them, and
makes our charity to them an all important element of
the Last Judgment.

Spiritual hunger, that is, the desire for the needs of
the soul, receives special attention in the Bible. "See
what days are coming, it is the Lord Yahweh who speaks,
days when I will bring famine on the country, a famine
not of bread but of hearing the word of God. They will
stagger from sea to sea, wander from north to east, seeking the word of Yahweh and failing to find it" (Am 8:11-
12). God is tired of speaking without being heard and no
longer sends prophets. Though the people may wander
all over the known earth seeking it, they will not find
the word of the Lord. A life solely nourished on the
sweetmeats of this world is soon stripped to the bone

when they are gone. Then comes the hunger for an authoritative spiritual word.

Our Lord proclaims a beatitude for the hungry. "Blessed are those who hunger and thirst after righteousness for they shall be satisfied" (Mt 5:6). "Blessed are you that hunger now for you shall be satisfied . . . Woe to you who are full now, for you shall hunger" (Lk 6:21, 25). Matthew's beatitudes are a formula for a virtuous life and they promise heavenly rewards. Luke speaks of material conditions in this life to be reversed in the next. The contrast between the present and the future lot of the godly is that between famine and feast. In Jewish and Christian imagery the good time coming is likened to a great feast. Luke speaks of real hunger; Matthew of spiritual, moral hunger. Righteousness is goodness or Christian perfection in its widest sense. It designates a condition of good relations with God, holy living achieved by submission to his will.

Those blessed humbly seek for what they believe is not yet theirs; the others, on the contrary, have the pride of believing that they lack for nothing, like the people at Laodicea. "You say to yourself, I am rich, I have made a fortune, and have everything I want, never realizing that you are wretchedly and pitiably poor, and blind and naked" (Rv 3:17). Laodicea was rich in worldly goods but spiritually poor. Riches have a blinding effect. The complacent and self-satisfied are really spiritually poverty-stricken. In the spiritual realm self-sufficiency means destitution.

Our Lord declares that the one who comes to him will satisfy his hunger, because he will find abundantly all spiritual benefits. "I am the bread of life. He who comes to me will never be hungry" (Jn 6:35). He is the living bread that supremely satisfies; all being and well-being reside in Christ, the Lord of life. Jesus himself is God's gift of spiritual sustenance for time and eternity, just as bread is the type of all earthly sustenance. What bread is to the body, Christ is to the soul. He alone knows the secrets of God and reveals them to men. The believer will experience the continual satisfaction of all his spiritual needs in Christ who is able to satisfy every aspiration after God and holiness. Believing in Christ is the only means of securing genuine, lasting spiritual satisfaction.

"The bread that I shall give is my flesh for the life of the world . . . anyone who eats this bread will live forever" (Jn 6:51-58). Jesus is the true bread because he is God's Word of revelation, but also because he is a victim whose body and blood are offered in sacrifice for the life of the world, and must be assimilated as such by the believer in the holy Eucharist. The eating effects the appropriation of the sacrifice. Eating and drinking Christ's flesh and blood is not the same thing as faith, though faith is the means of it. It results in an actual and vital union with Christ's human nature, whereby the believer dwells in Christ and Christ in him, and all the benefits of Christ's passion are communicated to him.

By the flesh of Christ is to be understood his human nature (Jn 1:14) and by his blood, his atoning blood shed for the sins of the world. This is a reference, therefore, to the Incarnation and to the Redemption. The eating and drinking of Christ's flesh and blood is real but spiritual (6:63) and can only take place through the medium of faith (6:35, 40, 47). It is not, however, identical with faith, but rather is the reward of faith. Those who have lively faith in Christ as the Son of God and the Redeemer of the world, are so incorporated with him, that they dwell in him and he in them (56); he is in them a principle of spiritual life (57) and of resurrection (54); and he strengthens and refreshes their souls, so that they neither hunger nor thirst (35, 55) as they experience even here below a foretaste of everlasting life (50, 51, 54, 58). This vital union between Christ and the believer, the main effect of eating his body and drinking his blood, is illustrated elsewhere by the allegory of the True Vine (Jn 15:1-17), and by St. Paul's metaphor of the body and the members (1 Cor 12:12-30).

The Lord's Supper was ordained as the ordinary and covenanted means of feeding upon Christ, that is, of appropriating spiritually but really and by faith, his glorified humanity, and sharing in the benefits of his passion and resurrection. Thus the original apostolic doctrine safeguards both the reality of the reception by the believing soul of Christ's true humanity, and also the absolute need of a lively faith if this blessed result is to be achieved. The Evangelist emphasizes the reality of Christ's flesh or human nature, and of his blood or atoning sacrifice; he also stresses the need of a living faith, as the only means through which Christ's flesh and blood can be savingly appropriated and become the food of our soul.

About wisdom it is written: "They who eat me will hunger for more" (Si 24:29). Unlike material food which soon satiates, surfeits, destroys interest and desire, and results in disgust, wisdom is perfectly satisfying yet never disgusts. The appetite for wisdom grows by what it feeds on. Jesus says: "I am the bread of life, he who comes to me will never be hungry" (Jn 6:35). Our Lord stresses the satisfying character of his gift of heavenly bread, which also, like wisdom, activates the soul's desires but also completely satisfies every spiritual aspiration and forever, since the life Jesus gives is eternal life.

3.

WATER AND THIRST

Water, one of the most necessary, common, and salutary elements in nature, along with drought, want of rain, and thirst, its consequence, all play an important part in the Bible presentation of divine revelation.

Meetings at wells are a feature of the patriarchal narratives (Gn 24:11, 29:2). Wells and springs play a significant part in the life and religion of the patriarchs (Gn 26:15, Ex 15:22-27). In the Old Testament spring water symbolizes the life that God gives, especially that of the Messianic age.

The march of the Israelites through the wilderness is punctuated with the theme of the complaints of Israel about thirst, hunger, and the dangers of war. "Tormented by thirst the people complained about Moses. Yahweh said to him: You must strike the rock and water will flow from it for the people to drink. This is what Moses did in the sight of the elders of Israel" (Ex 17:3-7). "Water gushed in abundance, and the community drank and their cattle too" (Nb 20:11). This miracle is often referred to in various biblical passages. Psalms 78 and 106 give the history of Israel mainly as resistance to the advances of God's grace. Israel is a restive people and rejects even God's blessings. Other writers stress rather God's kindness: "Those he led through the deserts never went thirsty; he made water spring from the rock, he split the rock and water flowed."

At the time of the exile, thirst is one of the evils that

strike the unfaithful Israelites. "You will submit to the
enemies that Yahweh will send against you in hunger,
thirst, nakedness, and utter destitution" (Dt 28:48). "I will
make a wilderness of her, turn her into an arid land, and
leave her to die of thirst" (Ho 2:3). "They have abandoned me, the fountain of living water" (Jr 2:13).

The prophets of the exile elaborate the theme of the
renewal of the miracles of the Exodus. "The poor and
needy ask for water and there is none, their tongue is
parched with thirst. I, Yahweh, will answer them; I, the
God of Israel, will not abandon them. I will make rivers
well up on barren heights, and fountains in the midst of
valleys; turn the wilderness into a lake, and dry ground
into watersprings" (Is 41:17-18). The new Exodus will be
more marvelous than the old. Yahweh gave water to his
people in the wilderness; now the wilderness itself is
watered and God's abounding favor makes it a new Eden.
This symbolic fertility is characteristic of the Messianic
era, of which the return from exile is itself a presage
(Ezk 47:1-12).

Israel's sages also use water as a sapiential theme.
Water symbolizes the life imparted by divine wisdom
and by the law. "The wise man's teaching is a life-giving
fountain" (Pr 13:14). The law gives the water of wisdom
to drink (Si 15:3). In Si 24:23-29, the law is compared to
the great rivers of Paradise and to the Jordan, fertilizing
the land with their abundant waters.

Just as thirst is a natural image for frustration: "like
the thirsty man who dreams he drinks and wakes ex-
hausted, his throat parched" (Is 29:8); so also, water is
used as a pleasant image: "Cold water to a thirsty throat,
such is good news from a distant land" (Pr 25:25). The
Psalmist tells God: "With you is the fountain of life"
(Ps 36:9); life stands for prosperity, peace, happiness. The
fountain of life in Pr 13:14 is wisdom and the fear of the
Lord in Pr 14:27.

The need to satisfy thirst is so basic and humane that already the Old Testament morality specified: "If your enemy is thirsty give him something to drink. By this you heap red-hot coals on his head, and Yahweh will reward you" (Pr 25:21-22). The best way to take vengeance on one's enemy is to be merciful to him, to make him feel ashamed by meeting evil with good. Kindness should provoke burning pangs of shame and lead to repentance. And in any case God rewards kindness. The best way to get rid of an enemy is to turn him into a friend. This advice is taken up by St. Paul (Rm 12:20) who just repeats, having nothing further to add.

Our Lord taught that even the smallest act of kindness to his disciples because they bear his name, is truly significant. "If anyone gives a cup of cold water to one of these little ones, because he is a disciple, then I tell you most solemnly, he will most certainly not lose his reward" (Mt 16:42). Even a simple deed of kindness, a very small act of service will be noted by God and rewarded. Our Lord goes further and states (Mt 25:31-46) that we will be judged by our works of mercy rather than by any occasional exploit (Mt 7:22). One of the works of mercy specified is the relief of thirst. "I was thirsty and you gave me to drink . . . Lord, when did we see you thirsty and give you to drink? . . . In so far as you did it to the least of my brethren you did it to me" (Mt 25:35, 37, 40). There is no substitute for active love. Jesus makes the rank-and-file brother in need his representative, he identifies himself with him. Whatever is done for Christ's sake is done through Christ's grace.

The Evangelists, John in particular, feel no difficulty about ascribing normal human emotions and physical needs to Jesus. "Jesus, tired by the journey, sat down at the well. When a Samaritan woman came to draw water, Jesus said to her, Give me a drink" (Jn 4:6-7). His fatigue and thirst underline the reality of his humanity.

John displays characteristic irony in representing the giver of living water himself thirsty and in need of a drink.

Jesus, as soon as he arrived at Golgotha and before he was crucified, was offered some wine mixed with myrrh (Mk 15:23). The drink was apparently meant as an anaesthetic to help the condemned to endure the pain of being nailed to the cross. Mt 27:34 reports that Jesus tasted this wine but refused it. He describes the wine as being mixed with gall, probably to establish a reference to Ps 69:21: "For food they gave me gall and for my thirst vinegar." The psalmist is describing a hostile action, which is suggested by Lk 23:36.

A second drink was offered to Jesus on the Cross at his death. "After this Jesus knew that everything had now been completed, and to fulfill the scripture perfectly he said, I am thirsty." The fatigue which he had undergone, the grief he felt, the heat of the day, and the loss of blood were the natural causes of this thirst. "A jar full of vinegar stood there, so putting a sponge soaked in the vinegar on a hyssop stick, they held it up to his mouth." Vinegar is the cheap sour wine in common use at the time as a thirst quencher. "After Jesus had taken the vinegar he said, 'It is accomplished;' and bowing his head he gave up his spirit" (Jn 19:28-30). He accepted the sympathetic gesture of the Roman soldiers. He had refused the stupefying draught which would have clouded his faculties; he accepts what will revive them for the effort of a willing surrender of his life. The literal sense must not be lost. Thirst was one of the worst agonies of crucifixion. Christ's words of human anguish again attest to his true humanity.

Given the Johannine love for symbolism one might also see in our Lord's thirst an expression of his desire to go to God and to assure the salvation of the world.

There could also be here a touch of Johannine irony: Jesus is the source of living water (Jn 4:38) yet cries out in thirst. He thus signifies that he must die before the living water can be given; and in the next episode water will pour forth from his corpse (Jn 19:34). Perhaps the most prominent symbolism is relative to Jn 18:11: "Am I not to drink the cup the Father has given me?" The cup was one of suffering and death; and now having finished his work, Jesus thirsts to drink that cup to the last drop, for only when he has tasted the bitter wine of death will his Father's will be fulfilled. Finally, the mention of hyssop may be symbolically evocative of Jesus' dying as the paschal lamb of the new covenant. In Egypt the blood of the lamb sprinkled by means of hyssop spared the Israelites from destruction (Ex 12:22). Jesus dies as the Lamb of God who takes away the world's sin (Jn 1:29).

Following the example of the Old Testament thinkers, Jesus also uses the word thirst figuratively to express the need or great desire that one has for something, especially the needs of the human soul for something higher and more satisfying than it could discover in its earthy experiences. Isaiah 55:1 is an invitation to partake in a symbolic messianic banquet, in the spiritual blessings of the new covenant. "O come to the water all who are thirsty; though you have no money, come! Buy at no cost wine and milk." The imagery gains point from the preciousness of water sold in the streets. The divine bounty will go beyond the bread and water of the wilderness to the wine and milk of the promised land. The only condition is a thirst for God. The Bible often evokes the banquet symbol to describe God's love which cannot be purchased. This call of abounding grace is unsurpassed for warmth and welcome even in the New Testament. The paradox of buying without money throws into relief the twin facts of sure possession and total dependence which are implied in grace; the union of the undoubting and the undeserving (Heb 4:16).

The psalmist uses the figure of thirst to express his love for the temple and for God's presence there. "As a doe longs for running waters, so longs my soul for you, my God. My soul thirsts for God, the God of life" (Ps 42:1-2). Our Lord proclaims, "Blessed are those who thirst after righteousness, for they shall be satisfied" (Mt 5:6). He who seeks the graces of the kingdom of God will be speedily and effectually blessed or satisfied.

To the Samaritan woman, "Jesus replied: Whoever drinks this water will get thirsty again; but anyone who drinks the water that I shall give will never be thirsty again; the water that I shall give will turn into a spring inside him, welling up to eternal life" (Jn 4:13-14). Living, spring water in the Old Testament signifies divine vitality, revelation, wisdom. It is the reality of which Jacob's well is but a symbol. It is a spring welling up permanently within a man, making him a new creature. It would be a mistake to try to tie John to one particular symbolic interpretation. The metaphor is intended to be very inclusive.

In Jn 3:16 Jesus himself is God's gift and this gift is the medium to eternal life to all who truly believe. God's bounty is Jesus himself. The spiritual thirst which God implanted within man is quenched by the gift of spiritual life of which Jesus knew himself to be the channel. He was conscious in the depth of his being of a source of life which had its fount in God; and he believed himself to be the mediator of the vital energies of God to men.

More specifically, living water is the revelation which Jesus gives to men; it is Jesus' teaching and revelation about God. The use of living water in this sense is paralled elsewhere in John by the use of the symbols of light

(Jn 8:12) and of the bread of life (6:27) with the same meaning. Living water for John is also the Spirit communicated by Jesus (Jn 7:37-39), the Spirit of truth, the agent who interprets Jesus' revelation to men (Jn 14:26, 16:13). The living water must also be the grace and truth of which Jesus is full (Jn 1:14) and which is communicated to believers through the Spirit. It is an inner principle of spiritual life which is not bound by the limits of earthly existence. It is what results from the new birth from above (Jn 3:3-8). To describe it with the metaphor of an internal fountain, gushing up inexhaustively, is to suggest something of the richness of the new life that is made available through faith in Christ. In Jn 3:5-8 the Spirit is the controlling influence over the whole life of those who participate in eternal life through incorporation into Christ. The metaphor of water suggests what this influence produces: a flow of thoughts and words and actions which accord with God's will and inspiration and continue into eternal life. As water quenches the thirst, refreshes and invigorates the body, purifies things defiled and renders the earth fruitful, so it is an apt emblem of the gift of the Holy Spirit which so satisfies the souls that receive it that they thirst no longer for earthly goods; it purifies also from all spiritual defilement, on which account it is emphatically styled the Holy Spirit; and it makes those who receive it fruitful in every good work.

"On the last and greatest day of the festival, Jesus stood there and cried out: 'If any man is thirsty, let him come to me. Let the man come and drink who believes in me!' As Scripture says: From his breast shall flow fountains of living water" (Jn 7:37-38). The liturgy of the feast of Tabernacles which formed the background of these words included prayers for rain, rites that commemorated the Mosaic water-miracle, and readings from biblical passages foretelling the benefits of the Messianic

era. For seven days water was carried from the Pool of
Siloam to the Temple and poured forth, as a reminder
of the water from the rock in the desert (Nb 20:2-13) and
as a symbol of hope for the Messianic deliverance (Is
12:3). Jesus is the true water of life (Jn 6:35) who turns
the symbol (Is 55:1) into reality. He is able to satisfy
every aspiration after God and holiness. The one who
believes in him experiences the continual satisfaction of
his highest spiritual needs.

During the climax of the celebration of Tabernacles,
Jesus stood in the temple court to proclaim solemnly that
he is the source of living waters. Ze 14:8 had predicted
that living waters would flow out of Jerusalem and Ezk
47:1 had seen a river flow from the rock underneath the
Temple. But now Jesus says that these rivers of living
water will flow from his own body, that body which is
the new Temple (Jn 2:21). In the desert wanderings which
the feast recalled, Moses had satiated the thirst of the
Israelites by striking a rock from which he brought forth
rivers of living water (Ps 78:16). Now those who thirst
need only to come to Jesus and through belief in him the
water of life will be theirs.

Here again the symbolism of the living water is multiple, as above; it is especially a figure of the Spirit given
by the risen Jesus. "He was speaking of the Spirit which
those who believe in him were to receive; for there was
as yet no Spirit because Jesus had not yet been glorified"
(Jn 7:39). Wisdom and the Torah personified as water
are sapiential commonplaces. Symbolic action combines
with sapiential adage to make a sign which for Christians
stands for Jesus, Wisdom in Person, and for the element
into which they were baptized, to drink with deep and
lasting satisfaction from union with the living God. Thus
this Christian midrash summarizes the prophetic significance of the Mosaic miracle. Christ, the spiritual Rock
(1 Cor 10:4) and the Temple, is the source of the waters

of the Spirit, from which the people of God drink. As a true spring is ever supplied with water from the great deep with which it has communication, so shall the soul of the genuine believer be supplied with light, life, love, and liberty and all other graces of the indwelling Spirit from the indwelling Christ.

Finally, the blood of Jesus is presented as the unusual drink of the Christian disciple. "If you do not drink the blood of the Son of Man, you will not have life in you. Anyone who does drink my blood has eternal life. For my blood is real drink. He who drinks my blood lives in me and I live in him" (Jn 6:51-56). Blood is part of the Eucharistic symbolism and stands for Christ's redemptive death which is made available to us in the Eucharistic mystery.

4.

MEALS IN THE OLD TESTAMENT

The Hebrew language has no special word for a meal. To express the idea of partaking of an ordinary meal it says simply to eat bread (Gn 37:25); a festive meal or banquet is a drinking, of wine understood.

Taking a meal together has always been a sign of friendship and hospitality. It is then not surprising that in his primitive religious consciousness, man should seize upon the experience of a meal to express his desire for union with the deity. There are consequently in the Bible, both meals of human fellowship and meals of religious communion. All meals, both secular and sacred, express a fundamental reality of human existence, our solidarity in life, with our fellow man in profane meals, and with God in sacred meals. In both there is a recognition of the reality of life as a common possession, and the meal celebrates this life in joy and thanksgiving. Meals celebrate the sharing of human life as a gift from God, and in this they anticipate the perfect sharing which Christ exemplified when he instituted the Eucharist at the Last Supper.

The biblical symbolism of the ordinary meal provides an opportunity to observe the transition from the ordinary meal to the sacred meal, as well as the characteristics of the sacred meal. An ordinary meal was the sign of a joyful reunion (Tb 7:9, Lk 23-32), of courtesy and hospitality (Gn 24:33, 54) even towards a stranger (Lk 24:29-30), and of thanksgiving to God (Gn 14:18-19).

It was a very natural custom to conclude all the most
significant celebrations of human life with a banquet or a
repast of some kind, for example, marriages or funerals.
But especially the important interventions of God in salvation history include a meal; for example, the appari-
tion at Mamre with the promise of the birth of Isaac (Gn
18:1-15). The passage gives a fine description of Oriental
courtesy and hospitality. "Abraham hastened to the tent
to find Sarah. 'Hurry,' he said, 'knead three bushels of
flour and makes loaves.' Then running to the cattle Abraham took a fine and tender calf and gave it to the servant,
who hurried to prepare it. Then taking cream, milk and
the calf he had prepared, he laid all before them, and
they ate while he remained standing near them under
the tree" (Gn 18:6-8). Abraham plays the part of the
lavish and deferential host in the best tradition of Oriental hospitality, the virtue most prized by the ancient
Semite.

In the desert the love of God was manifested by providing the people with the manna. This probably refers
to so-called honey-dew found on some local shrub. In any
case, the narrative (Ex 16) asserts some special intervention by which God fed his people. "Moses said to them,
It is the bread which the Lord has given you to eat" (Ex
16:15). The Psalms and the Book of Wisdom gratefully
record the gift of the manna which in Christian tradition,
as early as Jn 6:26-58, is a figure of the Eucharist, the
spiritual food of the Church, the new Israel, during our
earthly Exodus. St. Paul calls manna "spiritual food"
and regards it as a type of the Lord's Supper wherein the
faithful are partakers of the life that is in Christ (1 Cor
10:3-4).

The promised land is described as one "where milk
and honey flow" (Ex 3:8), a description frequent in the
Pentateuch, a proverbial expression denoting great fertility of soil and abundance, exquisiteness of food. Milk

and honey were and still are favorite foods in the East. The promised land is thus presented as a paradise in the eyes of the semi-nomads accustomed to the desert with its brief spring grazing.

It was a regular custom to ratify treaties and solemn agreements between various men or between God and man with a common meal, symbolizing a sharing of life and a union of joy. The meal becomes sacred because it externalizes the faith of the participants that God is the source of life and joy that binds them together. God sanctions and witnesses a covenant between men; the meal is considered as being taken in his presence. In Gn 31:54 a treaty is struck between Jacob and Laban. "Jacob offered a sacrifice on the mountain and invited his brothers to the meal. They ate the meal and passed the night on the mountain." It was believed that the deity was present at the covenant meal. In Ex 18:12 by offering sacrifice Jethro acknowledges Yahweh as God. By inviting Aaron and the elders to the sacred meal which follows the communion sacrifice, he strengthens his family ties with Israel. The covenant on Sinai is confirmed by a sacrificial meal in the presence of God. "They saw the God of Israel beneath whose feet there was, it seemed, a sapphire pavement pure as the heavens themselves. He laid no hand on these notables of the children of Israel; they ate and drank" (Ex 24:10-11). The sacrificial meal symbolized the harmonious relationship existing between the offerers and God. God does not appear as previously with terror-inspiring accompaniments of thunder, lightning, and smoke (20:18-19) but in grace and mercy. Far from being consumed, they feast in God's presence in the glory of unsurpassing beauty.

The **Passover meal** (Ex 12) was the most important of all the Old Testament sacred meals. The Passover was first an old pastoral feast consisting of a springtime night sacrifice to secure protection against evil powers. It in-

sured the fecundity of the flock, and through the blood
smeared on the tentpoles it warded off hostile or evil
powers. It was probably celebrated just before the shepherds moved out of their winter grazing grounds into
greener regions which provided pasture during the dry
season. The feast of Unleavened Bread (Massot) was originally an agricultural feast celebrating the beginning of
the barley harvest; an offering was made of the first-
fruits of the harvest. Unleavened bread was prescribed
so that the product of the new harvest would not be con-
taminated by any remnant from the old crop. These two
feasts were united and historicized, that is, charged with
the great event of the deliverance of God's people from
Egypt, and thus given a fresh salvific significance. The
sprinkling with blood now recalled the death of the first-
born of the Egyptians, while the unleavened bread was
referred to the haste of the departure of the Israelites.

The Jewish Passover prepared the Christian Pasch:
Christ is the Lamb of God, immolated on the cross, and
eaten at the Last Supper in the background of the Jewish
Passover. He thus brings salvation to the world, and the
mystical re-enactment of his act of redemption becomes
the focus of our Christian liturgy which centers around
the sacrificial meal of our Eucharistic celebration.

For the Christian the Paschal Lamb is a type of Christ.
The lamb is one of the most significant of John's symbols
for Christ (Jn 1:29; Rv 5:6, 12). It blends the idea of the
servant (Is 53) who takes on himself the sins of men and
offers himself as a lamb of expiation (Lv 14), with that
of the Passover lamb whose ritual symbolizes Israel's
redemption. This description of the Messiah contrasts
with the prevalent Jewish idea of a conqueror who would
restore the kingdom of Israel. The Jews generally regarded the Messiah not as the Lamb of God but as the
Lion of the tribe of Judah. Jesus is a Savior offering a
new and better sacrifice for sin, a Savior who annuls the

guilt of the whole human race. All lambs which had been hitherto offered had been furnished by men; this one is furnished by God, as the only sufficient and available sacrifice for the sins of the world.

"Christ, our Passover, has been sacrificed; let us celebrate the feast, then, by getting rid of the old yeast of evil and wickedness, having **only the unleavened bread of sincerity and truth**" (1 Cor 5:7-8). At Passover, according to the Jewish ritual, all leavened bread was removed from the houses (Ex 15:15), the Paschal Lamb was immolated (Ex 12:6), and only unleavened bread was eaten. These were symbolic preparations for the Christian mystery. Christ is our Paschal Lamb, the effective sign of our liberation from the bondage of sin. The figure expresses the sacrificial and redemptive aspects of his death. By his sacrifice, Christ the true Paschal Lamb destroys the old leaven of sin and makes possible a pure and holy life, symbolized by unleavened bread. The Christian is united with the sacrificed and risen Christ in an unending Passover; he must therefore remove the old yeast, evil and wickedness, and use instead unleavened bread, sincerity and truth, single-mindedness or purity of intention. Our new life is a continuing festival of thanksgiving and communion. The Church is always engaged in a Paschal celebration, because Christ by his death and resurrection has accomplished the salvation foreshadowed in the Exodus and makes it available to us in the Eucharist.

The first-born of all creation, the Lamb of God without blemish, was offered once for all on the cross. In the Eucharist we plead this sacrifice, we realize our unity with each other, we renew our communion with God, and the atoning virtue of the blood of the Lamb is applied for the salvation of all who by faith partake of the sacred feast. John 19:36 places the Crucifixion at the time of the immolation of the Paschal Lamb, and regards the fact

as significant. Christ's death redeems his people from
their spiritual bondage; his Eucharistic blood sprinkled
on our hearts delivers us from the guilt and consequences
of sin.

St. John finds symbolism in the fact that our Lord's
legs were not broken like those of the two thieves. "This
happened to fulfill the words of scripture: ' Not one bone
of his will be broken' " (19:36). Two texts are here com-
bined; one from Ps 34:20 describing how God protects
the virtuous man persecuted (Ws 2:18-20) of whom the
servant of Yahweh (Is 53) is the ideal example: "Hard-
ships in plenty beset the virtuous man, but Yahweh
rescues him from them all; taking care of every bone,
Yahweh will not let one be broken." A vivid figure for
complete preservation. There is also the ritual instruction
for the preparation of the Passover lamb: "Nor must you
break any bone of it" (Ex 12:46). The unity of the company keeping the feast is emphasized by the rules that
one lamb is to be eaten in one house, that no part of the
flesh is to be carried outside the house, and that no bone
of the lamb is to be broken. The unmutilated lamb symbolized the unity of Israel. St. John sees it as an emblem
of the unbroken bones of Christ. Jesus fulfills the Passover (1 Cor 5:7). He died as the true Paschal Lamb. The
ideal Lamb of God perfectly accorded with the ancient
sacrificial regulations. Jesus is the suffering, innocent
servant who takes on himself the sins of others; and even
if he is brought to slaughter like a lamb (Is 53:7), God
does not allow his bones to be broken; in his care for
him God will see to the victory of resurrection.

Along with the Passover, the **communion** sacrifice
(Lv 3), often called peace-offering, ranks high among
the sacred meals in the Bible. This sacrifice, it is thought,
represents the earliest form of sacrifice, in which the
deity and the worshipers exhibit their good relationship.
It is therefore the sacrifice expressive of harmony be-

tween God and his people. It is a feast of communion. It was a sacred banquet at which the worshipers ate one portion of the victim; the other portion, the blood and fatty parts considered as being most vital, was made over to the deity. It seems to have been the most commonly celebrated sacrifice in ancient Israel and the central rite of her feasts. Since it was a meal shared with God, it expressed better than any other sacrifice the union of God with his faithful. It was a covenant meal in which the worshiper was sacramentally related to God and to fellow Israelites. Of all forms of sacrifice this bears the closest analogy to the sacrament of the Eucharist. One of its key elements is the notion of life sharing between God and his faithful.

Peace offerings were made after a victory (1 S 11:15), before battle (1 S 13:9), at the introduction of the ark to Jerusalem (2 S 6:17), at the halting of the plague (2 S 24:25), at the installation of Solomon (1 K 3:15), at the consecration of the Nazarite (Nb 6:14), at the consecration of the Temple (1 K 8:64), with the morning burnt offering (Ezk 46:2), and other regular occasions, "new moons and sabbath, for all solemn festivals of the house of Israel" (Ezk 45:17).

According to the ideas of the ancients, the consumption of a part of the offering by the giver himself, effected a union and fellowship between him and the deity, who by accepting the other part of the offering showed his willingness to enter into this fellowship. To obtain this communion with God is also the purpose of other rites like the offerer placing his hand on the sacrifice (Lv 1:4) to signify that the victim takes his place, or the sprinkling of both the altar and the people with the same sacrificial blood, as was done at the ratification of the Sinai Covenant (Ex 24:3-8), to symbolize the union between God and his people.

In a passage written against self-indulgence, Amos

gives an idea of what the ancient profane banquet was like. "Lying on ivory beds and sprawling on their divans, they dine on lambs from the flock, and stall-fattened veal; they bawl to the sound of the harp, they invent new instruments of music like David, they drink wine by the bowlful, and use the finest oil for anointing themselves" (6:4-7). Elaborate furniture and sumptuous meals, musical entertainment with orgiastic refreshments: bowls instead of cups or goblets suggest excess.

The prophets began to use the banquet theme to announce the wondrous happiness in store for God's elect. Later the sages in Israel make their own application of this theme to the joy awaiting the virtuous man (Pr 9:1-3).

"On this mountain, Yahweh Sabaoth will prepare for all peoples a banquet of rich food, a banquet of fine wines, of food rich and juicy, of fine strained wines" (Is 25:6). Starting from this text, the idea of the Messianic banquet became current in Judaism and passed into the New Testament (Mt 22:2-10; Lk 14:14; 16-24). The image of a celestial banquet is given as a symbol of eternal happiness. Like a king holding his coronation feast, the Lord of hosts gathers all nations on Mount Zion for a rich feast with the best wine, fully matured, old wine full of flavor. The feast being a celebration suggests achievement, plenty, and shared delight. Our Lord relished this prospect even as he handed a very different cup, the Eucharist, to his disciples: "I shall not drink wine until the day I drink the new wine with you in the kingdom of my Father" (Mt 26:29).

5.

MEALS IN THE NEW TESTAMENT

Meals played a very important role in the life and teaching of our Lord. Jesus frequently appears at table and his table-fellowship became a central feature of his ministry, and the occasion and background of much of his teaching.

There is a whole theology involved in the meals taken by Jesus, as indicated in the New Testament; they symbolize the entire redemptive work he came to accomplish. Although he was poor and preached renunciation, Jesus made no radical departure from the usual life of the people of his time. By sharing meals with his disciples and other people, he showed first of all that he entered totally into our human existence, eating and drinking like the rest of us to sustain his human life. And since table-fellowship implies communion of life and acceptance of others, the meals of Jesus with sinners and outcasts clearly manifested the new era of forgiveness and reconciliation which he was inaugurating.

Jesus often sat at table, fraternized with disreputable people, the outcasts of society. The publican Levi's first missionary activity was to entertain Jesus in his house and invite his colleagues and acquaintances to meet Jesus. "When Jesus was at dinner at his house, a number of tax collectors and sinners were also sitting at table with Jesus and his disciples; for there were many of them among his followers" (Mk 2:15). The eagerness of the irreligious and immoral to listen to the most exacting of all teachers of religion and morality is very striking. They realized that he cared for them and believed in them enough to make his enormous demands upon them, and to bring to them his own perfect gift of understanding and sympathy. They felt encouraged by his kindness to better themselves.

The meal table is regarded in the East as the place of very close fellowship, a most intimate kind of personal contact. Jesus treated people as individuals not as stereotypes. "When the Pharisees saw this, they said to his disciples, Why does your master eat with tax collectors and sinners?" (Mt 9:11). In another passage they say: "Look, a glutton and a drunkard, a friend of tax collectors and sinners" (Mt 11:9). He is called a glutton and a drunkard as if he enjoyed low company for its own sake. "When he heard this he replied, It is not the healthy who need the doctor but the sick" (Mt 9:12). His reply is a model of common sense as well as a heartening expression of divine grace. But if Jesus did not condemn, neither did he condone; he came as Lk 5:32 interprets, to call sinners to repentance, as a physician heals the sick. Jesus' invitation to the Messianic banquet was extended not to the self-righteous but to repentant sinners. "Go and learn the meaning of the words: What I want is mercy not sacrifice. And indeed I did not come to call the virtuous but the sinners" (Mt 9:13). To the exact performance of the law's external demands God prefers the inward quality of genuine compassion. It is a favorite theme of the prophets (Am 5:21). Mercy means covenant love, a mutual relationship between God and his people defined by Hosea (6:6) as "the knowledge of God." On the basis of this conception of religion the Pharisees can only be called righteous ironically. Of course Christ came to call the Pharisees also, but they refused to be called, to accept the call. The message of Jesus is essentially redemptive, a message to the masses of the unwashed, ignorant, and erring. He is the physician of the sin-sick soul, and he looks for the response of confidence and committal. No more than a doctor could he be expected to keep his hands clean. His duty lay with the needy whom he invited to repent.

Luke 14:1 deserves special attention. This is one of the numerous cases when Jesus accepts entertainment in a Pharisee's house and enters into controversy. In eating and drinking people feel generally less restraint than at other times and are apt to converse more freely. "Now on a sabbath day he had gone for a meal to the house of one of the leading Pharisees; and they watched him very closely." It is interesting to note the easy access that Jesus had to the homes of important people. He knew the malice of the Pharisees but did not spurn them. He came to save the lost and to save he must seek.

The meals Christ attended often echo the characteristics of the Messianic age: joy (Mk 2:19), pardon (Lk 7:47), salvation (Lk 19:9). Our Lord's miracle of the multiplication of the loaves is a Messianic sign, an anticipation of the Messianic banquet of the time of fulfillment.

The miracle of the loaves is the only one found in all four gospels. That this story should have given rise to variant forms so early may indicate that it was very often told; and this in turn suggests that the connection of the story with the Eucharistic rite was present from the beginning. Luke (9:10-17) and John (6:1-15) tell of only one multiplication of loaves. Matthew (14:13-21, 15:32-39) and Mark (6:30-44, 8:1-10) report two. This is no doubt a very ancient (Mt 16:9-10) doublet which presents the same event according to two different traditions. The first, more archaic, of Palestinian origin seems to place the event on the west shore of the lake and mentions twelve baskets, the number of the tribes of Israel (Mk 3:14). It is a sign for the Jews. The second probably originated from Christians of pagan origin and places the event on

the east shore of the lake (Mk 7:31). It mentions seven
baskets, the number of the nations of Canaan (Ac 13:19)
and of the Hellenistic deacons (Ac 6:5, 21:8). It foreshadows the Eucharist as food for the gentiles. The two traditions describe the event in the light of the Old Testament
precedents, in particular the multiplication of the oil and
bread by Elisha (2K 4:1-7, 42-44) and of the episode of
the manna and the quails (Ex 16, Nb 11). Renewing with
superior power these gifts of heavenly nourishment, the
action of Jesus stands on its own and has been understood
by the most ancient tradition as a preparation for the
eschatological food par excellence, the Eucharist. This is
underlined by the literary presentation of the miracle in
the Synoptics and by the Johannine discourse on the
bread of life (Jn 6).

The incident is related less for the element of the
miraculous than as a symbol and anticipation of the
Eucharist and of the Messianic banquet (Mt 8:11-12).
This is evidenced by the liturgical and sacramental allusions incorporated into the form of the account. The ceremonial with which Jesus blesses and distributes the food
(Mt 14:19, 15:36) anticipates the Last Supper (Mt 26:26);
we find the same words in the same sequence; he took
bread, looked up, blessed, broke, gave. In Luke the episode constitutes a climax of Jesus' Galilean ministry, for
after that he concentrates upon the training of his apostles, with his thoughts centering upon his destiny. The
Eucharistic symbolism appears also in the manner in
which all four Evangelists link the multiplication of the
loaves with the announcement of the Passion, thus underlining the sacrificial feature of the Eucharist.

The association with the Eucharist is more explicit in
Jn 6, where the multiplication of the loaves is followed
by John's Eucharistic discourse. It is a Messianic sign
and symbol that will find its fulfillment in the true Messianic banquet, the Eucharist. In the light of John's ac-

count which leads on directly to the great discourse on the bread of life, we are left in no doubt as to the meaning of the story. Jesus is not only the giver of life; he is also the support and sustainer of it, as indispensable for Christian living as daily bread for the body, the complete satisfaction and nourishment of the believing soul who feeds upon him in his heart by faith.

Jesus' solicitude was not simply for the people's material hunger, but to represent to them the kingdom of God which could, if they would allow it, assuage their hunger for the things of the spirit. For Jesus the miracle of the loaves anticipates the eschatological Messianic banquet. It is a parable in action of the kingdom. It is this significance which the gospels develop in interpreting the miracle as a foreshadowing of the Eucharist, the Messianic banquet of the Church. As the multitudes had once enjoyed table-fellowship with Jesus as his guests by the Lake of Galilee, so now the Church enjoys table fellowship with the exalted Jesus in the Eucharist.

The meals of Jesus with his disciples were a sign of his sharing with them the mission which the Father gave him for the salvation of the world. This is very clearly stated in Christ's answer to the sons of Zebedee. "Can you drink the cup that I must drink, or be baptized with the baptism with which I must be baptized? They replied, 'We can.' Jesus said to them, "The cup that I must drink you shall drink, and with the baptism with which I must be baptized you shall be baptized" (Mk 10:38-39). The cup is a metaphor for one's lot in life, one's destiny. To drink the cup and to be baptized are symbols here of the approaching passion, in which Jesus is to be immersed in suffering. Christ's mission on earth is not to apportion men's rewards but to suffer for man's salvation (Jn 3:17). Fellowship with Christ in glory involves fellowship with him in suffering. The disciple can in some way take his part in Christ's work "and fill up what is lacking in

Christ's sufferings" (Col 1:24). Jesus suffered in order to
establish the kingdom of God, and anyone who continues
his work must share this suffering. This is part of the
way God always intended the Church to develop. Those
who are in Christ are caught up into his activity, and
though never able on their own merit to win their salvation, are by their very acceptance of this free gift brought
into the same stream of creative suffering. Until the end
of time the Church will be imperfect, in the sense that
it must continually develop both intensively and exten-
sively (Ep 4:10-13). In virtue of their baptism all Christians are called to contribute to filling up this gap between the actual and the potential, the real and the ideal.
They do this by living as authentic Christians which
inescapably involves suffering. Pain is always a condition of growth.

Jesus himself is the bread of life (Jn 6). Our sharing
in the new life which he came to give takes place through
the sign of a meal, the meal of the new covenant sealed
in his blood (1 Cor 11:25). In place of manna he gives his
own flesh as nourishment, the true living bread that
offers life to the world, everlasting life.

Following the lead of the Old Testament prophets (Is
25:6), our Lord often describes the final stage of salvation,
the perfect fulfillment of the new life he gives, as the
eschatological banquet. "I tell you, many shall come from
east and west to take their places with Abraham and
Isaac and Jacob at the feast in the kingdom of heaven"
(Mt 8:11). The Messianic deliverance is conceived as ad-
mission to a festive dinner prepared by God.

There is also our Lord's parable of the wedding feast,
the great supper (Mt 22:1-14). The king is God; the wedding feast is the happiness of the Messianic age; the king's
son is the Messiah; those sent with invitations are the
prophets and the apostles; the invited who ignore them
or do them violence are the Jews; those called in from

the street are the sinners and the pagans; the burning of
the city is the destruction of Jerusalem but in verse 11
the scene changes to the last judgment.

In Rv 3:20 the blessing Christ gives, the fellowship
of personal communion with him, is described as sharing
a meal with him. "If one of you hears me calling and
opens the door, I will come in to share his meal, side by
side with him." And the fifth beatitude in the book
describes the reward of the blessed: "Happy are those
who are invited to the wedding feast of the Lamb" (Rv
19:9).

It is in the context of these various biblical meals
that we find the meaning of the Last Supper which we
celebrate in the Eucharist. For Christ the Last Supper
was the culmination of a relationship that he was trying
to establish with his disciples, an expression of total, all-
embracing love (Jn 13:1). It was the last act that he performed in order to reveal the real meaning of his role as
our redeemer: an ardent love, deeply experienced and
expressed in the sign of a meal which he shared with
them on the night before he suffered; a committed love,
authentic to the core and manifested on the cross in an
act of self-gift. All the meals of men both profane and
religious find their fulfillment in this meal, because here
we have the perfection of human relationship, as well as
the initiation of man into the divine life.

The disciples experienced the love of their Master at
the Last Supper, but understood the full meaning of
their discipleship only after Pentecost. It is then that they
appear as the community of the risen Christ, and express
their community life in the ritual of the breaking of the
bread, but also in the practice of Christian fellowship,
by devoted care, especially for the poorer members of
the community (Ac 2:42-44). Since these apostolic days
the gathering together for the celebration of the Eucharist has been the life center and focus of the Christian

community. It was always the sign that distinguished the Christian community from other religious groups. Christians have always found their identity in the celebration of the Eucharistic meal, and by manifesting in their lives all that the sharing in such a meal implies. For Christ the Last Supper was the climax of his redemptive love; it was the sign of the gift of himself that he was to effect on the cross. For us the celebration of the Eucharist will truly be the distinguishing mark of our being a true Christian community when it is a sign of a love that unites us together, of a love that is committed to a life of devoted service.

The Eucharistic theology of Vatican II highlights this meal aspect of the Eucharist. "The Lord left behind a pledge of hope and strength for life's journey in that sacrament of faith where natural elements are changed into his glorified body and blood, providing a meal of brotherly solidarity and a foretaste of the heavenly banquet" (GS, no. 38). Because of the close connection that should exist between liturgy and life, the implications of the Eucharistic celebration under the sign of a meal have special significance for our times, when millions of people go without sufficient food daily. Christ's love for us was expressed in a meal at the Last Supper; if we are really animated by his love, we must learn to express it in the sharing of what we have with our brothers. Like the first Christians we must remain faithful to the teaching of the apostles, to sharing with our brothers, to the breaking of the Eucharistic bread, and to prayer (Ac 2:42).

6.

THE EUCHARIST AT CORINTH

First Corinthians 11:17-34 gives directions for the proper celebration of the Lord's Supper at Corinth, in view of correcting some prevalent disorders. This passage is especially important for it contains not only the oldest account of the institution of the Lord's Supper, written as much as ten years before Mark's, but also Paul's understanding of its significance.

Like other societies and guilds in Greek cities, the early Christian Church used to have a common meal, to which all contributed according to their means, the rich helping their poorer brethren. Being thus a token of brotherly love and Christian fellowship, the supper was called a Love Feast, an Agape. Like the celebration of the Last Supper, which had taken place in connection with a meal taken in common, in the earliest times, at least at Corinth, the Eucharist was connected with an Agape. Calling the Agape an ordinary meal would not be very appropriate since in the Oriental world, eating a meal with other people was a real sign of friendship and fellowship. Such was surely the meaning of the Christian communal meal. Later on, perhaps in consequence of such disorders as those here mentioned, the Eucharist was separated from the Agape.

The feast had been greatly abased by the selfishness and individualism so prevalent at Corinth. Each individual or small clique began at once to consume the food and wine brought, by themselves, without waiting for the whole community to assemble, and without letting the poorer brethren share with them. What ought to have been an evidence of brotherly love had become an exhibition of selfish greed; and under those circumstances it was impossible to have an orderly and reverent celebration of the Eucharist. St. Paul denounces this conduct (1 Cor 11:17-19). He blames the Corinthians for the divisions and abuses which desecrated their religious meetings and shows (20-22) how this spirit is fatal to the proper observance of the Lord's Supper. He reminds them of the institution and meaning of the Eucharist (23-26), of the need of partaking in a right spirit, and the sin and penalty of doing otherwise (27-32). He concludes with practical recommendations, which he will supplement when he comes (33-34).

"I hear that when you come together as a community, there are divisions among you, and I half believe it, since there must no doubt be factions among you, to distinguish those who are to be trusted" (1 Cor 11:18-19). The divisions were cliques perhaps corresponding to social classes at the supper, the richer members keeping to themselves instead of associating with the poorer Christians. Factions are unedifying but to some extent inevitable; so divine providence makes them serve a positive purpose. They expose men's true characters. Such divisions are a test of Christian faith.

"The point is, when you hold these meetings, it is not the Lord's Supper that you are eating, since when the time comes to eat, everyone is in such a hurry to start that one person goes hungry while another is getting drunk" (20-21). The richer Christians, who must have provided most of the food and drink for the meal, probably arrived at the meeting earlier than the others. The poorer members came later, after longer work hours, with their meager provisions. Some might even have been slaves, who were even less able to dispose of their

own time. The result was that each took care of himself;
some got too little, others too much and overindulged
even to the extent of drunkenness. In these circumstances it was not the Lord's Supper that was being eaten.
Even if they were performing the right actions and saying the correct words over the bread and wine, they were
not really concerned with what Christ meant by his actions at the Last Supper. They were concerned only with
the satisfaction of their own appetites. Their selfishness
was fatal to the proper spirit of devotion and brotherly
love; their supper became no more than an ordinary
meal. Paul calls this evening meal shared in common,
the Lord's Supper. The expression is found only here in
the New Testament. The meal is so called because it included the Eucharist in commemoration and renewal of
the great Last Supper celebrated by Jesus on Holy Thursday. The Corinthians celebrated the Eucharist in the setting of a meal which instead of being fraternal, resulted
not only in the breach of good manners but also in serious
abuses of charity, and even of the sacrament itself (29).
If the purposes of the Love Feast are abandoned, namely,
the expression of mutual love through the shared-out
food, culminating in the remembrance of Christ's great
act of love, then it is better to eat at home, and not show
contempt for the Church and indifference for the feelings
of the poor (22).

In marked contrast to the deplorable display of personal greed and humiliation of one's neighbor, to show
them how serious their ill-conduct is, Paul reminds the
Corinthians of what Jesus said and did, and what he
meant by commanding that the rite should be regularly
repeated. Paul makes straight for bed-rock. He recounts
the institution of the Lord's Supper. The Corinthians
fail to understand the spirit of perfect immolation, and
universal, infinite love which Christ manifested in the
institution of the Eucharist.

Paul taught them what he himself had been taught,
a tradition which stems from the words of Jesus himself
in the upper room. "This is what I received from the
Lord, and in turn passed on to you" (23). The Pauline
record of the words of institution of the Eucharist is very
similar to Lk 22:19-20, and probably represents the form
used in the Antiochene liturgy. That of Mark and Matthew probably represents the Jerusalem liturgical tradition. Though Paul's account provides documentary evidence earlier than that in the gospels, some scholars consider Mark's the most primitive on the basis that Paul's
tradition reflects the liturgical usage and perhaps the
sacramental associations of the Hellenistic Churches. On
the other hand some argue for the greater antiquity of
Paul's tradition, pointing to the lack of parallelism in the
bread and cup sayings in comparison with those of
Mark's version, which they judge to be an intermediate
step toward the exactly parallel formulas of the second
century Church. "On the night that he was betrayed, the
Lord Jesus took some bread, and thanked God for it and
broke it, and he said, This is my body, which is for you;
do this as a memorial of me" (24). The mention of the
betrayal calls to mind all the circumstances of the Passion, which we see St. Paul and his readers must have
fully known, and so gives force to Christ's last command,
and puts it in direct connexion with Christ's death on
the cross.

The word Eucharist means to pronounce a blessing,
to thank God, to utter the praise of God. It is closely
related to the idea of memorial or anamnesis, a rite for
remembrance which according to Jewish thought effects
what it recalls. This is one of the great aspects of the
Eucharist. This is how the Eucharistic food is consecrated
for us, by blessing God, the giver (1 Tm 4:4-5), as we
make remembrance of the death our Lord suffered to win
our redemption.

"Which is for you" can be taken to mean that Jesus died for our salvation (Rm 5:6-8), or that he died in our place (Gal 3:13). Because of the overtones of Is 52:13-53:12 in the expression, both of these ideas seem included. Liturgy is often pregnant with meaning.

In what sense is Christ present in the Eucharist, symbolically or realistically, in the bread and wine? What is the nature of the sacramental union of the believer with his Lord? Should one speak of this relationship as mystical or ethical? All efforts to restrict Paul's meaning to one or to the other of these, does violence to his understanding of the relation of Christ to men of faith, a union renewed with each faithful participation in the body and blood of Christ.

"In the same way he took the cup after supper, and said, This cup is the new covenant in my blood. Whenever you drink it, do this as a memorial of me" (25). The blood of Christ seals the new covenant, a new relationship between God and man, which was foretold in the Old Testament (Jr 31:31-32). Like the Sinaitic Covenant which was sealed with the blood of sacrificial victims (Ex 24:8), this is a pact in blood, one therefore marked by a sacrifice, which is both a sign of the pact and a cause of it, subordinate of course, to the primary causality which is God's. Christ's blood establishes a new covenant between God and man, one of forgiveness and grace. The cup is a seal or assurance of our being included within this covenant.

The Eucharist, at the center of which is Christ himself, contains the fulfillment of all the Old Testament expectations and the dawn of the eschatological hope. All the essential concepts of the Old Testament are gathered up in Christ's words of consecration: the covenant, the supreme authority of God, atonement and martyrdom, worship, and the eschatological message. Everything is centered in Christ, and through him God's activity in the matter of salvation is consummated and perfected. Everything that God has done in the past and everything that he wishes to accomplish in the future regarding man's salvation is incorporated in the Eucharist.

"Until the Lord comes, therefore, every time you eat this bread and drink this cup, you are proclaiming his death" (26). Paul goes on to emphasize the close relation between the Eucharist and the Cross, and the consequences which flow from that. "As often as" gives no directives as to how often, though a frequent remembrance is implied. In Acts 20:7 it was arranged for Sunday evening. Until the day of the Parousia, the Church proclaims the Lord's redemptive death when celebrating the Eucharist. It is the sacrament of the unseen presence, recalling the past death and pledging the future triumph. Paul stresses the sacrificial aspect of the sacrament as memorial and symbol of the Lord's death. Just as the Passover celebration commemorated the deliverance of Israel from Egyptian bondage (Ex 12:14) so the Eucharist commemorates the liberation brought about by Christ, the liberation from slavery to the devil and sin (Jn 19:36). The Eucharist is a living sermon, a perpetual proclamation of the death of Christ, not as an act of mourning, but as an occasion of living hope. The announcement is contained in the Eucharistic celebration, the meaning of which is known to the Christians; by their partaking of the Eucharist, they show their faith and proclaim its object, namely, the meaning of our Lord's salvific death and his resurrection. "Until he comes." The rite is to be repeated until Jesus returns at the Parousia; thus the rite also proclaims belief in the second coming of Jesus and in the general resurrection, when he will drink with them at the triumph feast (Mt 26:29).

The Eucharist is not a dramatic imitation of what was done at the Last Supper; it is the same thing. The relation of the Eucharist to the Last Supper is not simply in the way in which, for example, a scene in a pageant is related to the historical event which it depicts; it is that event re-enacted. The death of the Lord is actually present because Christ's body, sacrificed for his own in death, and his blood, shed for them in death, are both present. The eating of the bread and the drinking of the wine by the participant is a symbol that Christ's crucifixion and resurrection vitally affect their own individual lives. These actions, however, are more than a dramatic symbol. They are the actual means by which the results of the death of Christ become real and effective in the lives of his followers. They are the means by which each Christian is able to experience for himself the new relationship with God which the crucifixion made possible. The sacrament has some resemblance with Old Testament symbolic actions of the prophets (Jr 18:1). It expresses here and now the reality of something which actually took place at a different moment.

"And so anyone who eats the bread and drinks the cup of the Lord unworthily will be guilty of profaning the body and blood of the Lord" (27). This verse implies the doctrine of the real presence, suggested also by verse 29. The lack of love, the factious spirit, and the greed which Paul has been rebuking constitute an act of desecration. The guilt is not primarily against fellow-believers, great as that is, but against the person of Christ symbolized effectively in the elements.

A person should see whether he has the proper dispositions of faith and fraternal love required for worthy participation in the sacrament. "Everyone is to examine himself before eating this bread and drinking this cup; because a person who eats and drinks without recognizing the Body is eating and drinking his own condemnation" (28-29). He failed to recognize the sanctity of the body of Christ, the sacred meaning of the Eucharistic action. One must realize that it is not mere bread that is given under the symbol but the Lord's body, and while he partakes of it, he must also receive inwardly of Christ's spirit and increase in consciousness of union with him.

The condemnation is not eternal damnation but divine chastisement expressed physically in illness and death. "That is why many of you are weak and ill and some of you have died" (30). Paul considers the sickness and death of some of the Corinthians to have been a punishment for irreverence to the Eucharist. "If only we judged ourselves, we should not have been punished like that. But when the Lord does punish us like that, it is to correct us and stop us from becoming condemned with the world" (31-32). This divine visitation was medicinal and would have been avoided if the guilty had corrected their failings in their celebration of the Lord's Supper.

"So to sum up, my dear brothers, when you meet for the Meal, wait for one another. Anyone who is hungry should eat at home, and then your meeting will not bring your condemnation" (33-34). These are the correctives which together with the self-examination already demanded will create a proper atmosphere for the Lord's Supper. This is a time for togetherness; let them wait considerately for one another, and those who can't control their hunger should eat at home. Such is St. Paul's pastoral solution of a specific problem plaguing one of his favorite communities. It is the occasion of what is perhaps our most important material for a proper understanding of the Eucharistic mystery.

7.

THE EUCHARIST IN PAUL AND LUKE

St. Paul regards the Eucharist as a means of communion with Christ (1 Cor 10:16-17), a sign of brotherhood by which all Christians are united together (1 Cor 10:17), a memorial of Christ and of his death for man (1 Cor 11:24-26). He records Christ's words which describe the Eucharist as the seal of the New Covenant (1 Cor 11:25). From these Pauline passages we get the traditional phrases: Holy Communion, the Lord's Table, the Lord's Supper.

Notwithstanding its complications 1 Cor 10:2-4 also deserves a brief mention. In the context, before dealing with the problem of food sacrificed to idols, Paul quotes Old Testament history to remind the Corinthians of the danger of idolatry and so prevent them from joining in actual sacrificial meals (1 Cor 10:14-22). "I want to remind you, brothers, how our fathers were all guided by a cloud above them and how they all passed through the sea. They were all baptized into Moses in this cloud and in the sea" (1 Cor 10:1-2). The cloud denoted the presence of God and the passage through the Red Sea is made to suggest Christian baptism. "All ate the same spiritual food and all drank from the same spiritual drink, since they all drank from the spiritual rock that followed them as they went and that rock was Christ" (3-4). The Israelites also had a form, a sort of preview of the Lord's Supper. God took care of his people in the wilderness with miraculous food and drink.

Paul alludes to the legend that the rock from which Moses made water flow accompanied the Israelites on their travels through the wilderness. Rabbinical tradition had already tended to identify this rock with Yahweh himself. Paul sees it as a symbol of the pre-existent Christ already active in the history of Israel.

Paul employs the general terms for food and drink, the better to indicate their relation to the Eucharistic elements. This food and this drink were spiritual because they had a typical or spiritual, supernatural meaning (6). They were also spiritual in another sense, because they were not purely material, but miraculous, and because they came from the spiritual Rock (4), assuring the people of God's presence and strengthening their faith. The manna and the water from the rock, that never failed, are called spiritual because they were the result of a miracle, and because they prefigured the two elements of the Eucharist, the food and drink which Christ provides for the man regenerated by baptism. Like God who took care of his people in the wilderness, similarly the transfigured Christ, who is present in his Church, gives a new food and a new drink for the salvation of its members. They, God's people in exile, are provided for by their Lord. It emerges clearly from Paul's Christological appreciation of scripture and of history that he views the Eucharist as the nourishment of God's people of the New Testament, as the food for their journey. The rock of the Mosaic story becomes for Paul a symbol of the risen Christ who in the Eucharist refreshes the faithful in this life which is a journey to the land of his peace and glory.

1 Cor 10:14-22 is a warning against joining in the sacrificial meals of pagan worship. Remembering the rather liberal attitude expressed earlier (8:4-10), Paul warns against actual participation in pagan worship. To eat at a friend's table, or even at a banquet in a Temple,

food consecrated to an idol is one thing; taking part in a religious rite is quite another, and is comparable to the Lord's Supper in the Church. Paul calls the Eucharist, the cup of blessing. It is the cup of wine for which we bless God, thank him like Christ did at the Last Supper. The Lord's cup of blessing in turn is blessed by men, consecrated by thanksgiving and prayer, and so becomes a source of blessing. "The cup of blessing, is it not a communion with the blood of Christ, and the bread that we break, is not a communion with the body of Christ?" (16). In chapter 11 Paul presents the Eucharist under the aspect of Christ's death, here under that of communion with him; hence our term Holy Communion for this sacrament. Christ is invisibly present and through the symbolic action of his human representatives he makes available to each individual Christian the spiritual benefits which he secured in principle for the whole human race as a result of his death. The Church is spoken of as doing what was actually done by its president (Ac 20:11). Through eating the bread and drinking the cup, Christians are united to Christ in an intimate fellowship, a spiritual communion, because the Eucharist is his body and blood (11:27-31). From this Eucharistic fellowship with Christ follows the real union of all the faithful with one another in one body. Baptism incorporates the Christian into the body of Christ, the Eucharist strengthens and cements this union. The Eucharist is consequently "the sacrament of the unity of the Church" (St. Augustine), and when we receive the Eucharistic bread, Christ assimilates us and transforms us making us his own body.

"The fact that there is only one bread means that, though there are many of us, we form a single body because we all have a share in this one bread" (17). The Eucharist is the sacrament of unity in Christ. Sharers of the one Bread, broken and distributed to each, we all partake of Christ's body and are thus members incorpo-

rated into his mystical body, the blessed company of the
faithful people of God. "The many are one body" is Paul's
definition of the Church (Rm 12:5). There is mention of
bread and not wine because the solid food represents
better the unity intended.

Paul now draws a parallelism between Jewish and
pagan participation in their sacrifices through eating the
meat of the victims, and Christian fellowship with Christ
through the Eucharist. He clearly considers the eating of
the Eucharist a sacrificial repast and implies that the
Eucharist itself is a sacrifice. "Consider the practice of
Israel; are not those who eat the sacrifices in communion
with the altar?" (18). The Jew considers participation in
a sacrificial meal as fellowship with the altar, that is,
with the deity to whom the altar is consecrated and the
victim offered. He associates himself with all that the
altar signifies, and hence to God, whose worship is signified. Eating at pagan sacrificial feasts creates an analogous situation; the argument includes the pagan as well
as the Jew. "Does this mean that the food sacrificed to
idols has a real value or that the idol itself is real? Not
at all. It simply means that the sacrifices they offer, they
sacrifice to demons who are not God. I have no desire
to see you in communion with demons" (19-20). The
idols do not represent divinities for there is only one
God. But behind idolatry stand the evil spirits so that
as the Law says (Lv 17:7, Dt 32:17) the gentiles sacrifice
to demons. Idolatry is a medium through which satanic
power is particularly manifest (1 Jn 5:19, 21). "You cannot drink the cup of the Lord and the cup of demons.
You cannot take your share at the table of the Lord and
at the table of demons" (21). This is not a physical im-
possibility but the moral and spiritual incompatibility
of participation at the table of the Lord and the table
of demons.

Briefly, participation in the Eucharist establishes a

communion with the body and blood of Christ (16); the Old Testament victim places the participating Jews in communion with the altar (18); the food sacrificed to idols gives the pagan communion with demons (20). What was eaten in sacrificial meals was the flesh of victims offered on the altar. Paul states here that the "Eucharistized" bread and wine are parallel to these sacrificial meals, a statement he explains in the next chapter (11:24-27). The Eucharist is the blood of Christ, the body of Christ (1 Cor 10:16), the cup of the Lord (Kyrios), the table of the Lord (21), the Lord's Supper (1 Cor 11:20), the body of the Lord (29). Kyrios is the Lord in glory, the risen Lord. Paul is at pains to strengthen the attitude of reverence which ought to be present at the celebration of the Eucharist. The table of the Lord (Ml 1:7-12, Ezk 41:42, 44:16) is a sacrificial table, one on which ritual meals are consumed. The Christians possess the true sacrifice and the true sacrificial meal. The Eucharist is the only true form of worship for the new era.

The account which Paul gives of the Last Supper (1 Cor 11:17-34) in his correction of the abuses which were taking place in Corinth concerning its celebration, provides for the regulation of the form of public worship and the ordering of moral life and of the community. This is even more pronounced in Luke's account of the Last Supper (22:7-38). The celebration of the Eucharist is depicted as an event which is integrally woven into the fabric of the life of the community, and must be completely impenetrated by the moral life of the faithful, so that both the religious worship and the moral life of each individual form a single entity within the community.

St. Luke's account resembles most the liturgical tradition reproduced by St. Paul in 1 Cor 11:23-25; this is quite natural since he was a disciple of St. Paul. Luke combines two traditions, one a farewell testament (22:

15-18) and the other a liturgy of the institution of the Eucharist (19-20). The tradition of farewell probably comes from a Johannine circle that sought to understand the significance of what the Master did at the Last Supper with the twelve. In Luke, Christ's discourses at the Last Supper (22:14-15, 24-30, 35-38) play a more important part than in Mark or Matthew, preparing us for those in John (chs. 13-17). Luke seems to have conceived these discourses in the light of the primitive Christian assemblies. In Mark and Matthew the Eucharist is in the foreground. Luke's literary construction is dominated by a theological idea: the Eucharist is the Christian Passover (Lk 22:15-18). Our Lord is drinking a toast to the future.

"When the hour came he took his place at table, and the Apostles with him. And he said to them, I have longed to eat this passover with you before I suffer; because I tell you, I shall not eat it again until it is fulfilled in the kingdom of God. Then taking a cup, he gave thanks and said, Take this and share it among you, because from now on I tell you, I shall not drink wine until the kingdom of God comes" (14-18). This is the last time he is eating the Passover with his disciples, and the Paschal banquet is being fulfilled, realized, and replaced eminently by the Eucharist. Luke distinguishes the Passover and the cup of verses 15-18 from the bread and the cup of verses 19-20, in order to draw a parallel between the ancient rite of the Jewish Passover and the new rite of the Christian Eucharist. Some ancient authorities, failing to understand this theological device, and disturbed to find two cups mentioned, quite mistakenly omitted what is lacking in the shorter Lucan text which omits 19b and 20. In Mark 14:29 and Matthew 26:25 the outlook is purely eschatological with Eucharistic connotations. Luke suggests that the domain in which the new Paschal rite will find expression is the Church. The

Eucharist is the anticipation of the heavenly Messianic banquet. Jesus probably explained both aspects, the Eucharist in the Church (Luke) and the transcendent kingdom (Mark and Matthew), in more abundant terms.

"Then he took some bread and when he had given thanks, broke it and gave it to them, saying, This is my body which will be given for you; do this as a memorial of me. He did the same with the cup after supper, and said, This cup is the new covenant in my blood which will be poured out for you" (19-20). Jesus announces his approaching death and presents it as a sacrifice, like that of the victims whose blood sealed the Sinai covenant (Ex 24:5-8), but a redemptive sacrifice. For in speaking of the blood poured out for us in view of a new covenant, Jesus had in mind the servant of Yahweh whose life was to be poured out and who was to bear the sins of the multitude (Is 53:12). God gives the Servant as a covenant to the people and a light to the nations (Is 42:6); Jesus inaugurates the new covenant which Jr 31:31-34 had foretold. "Do this in remembrance of me" does not mean a mere commemoration but the renewal of a rite by means of which the sacrifice of the living Christ is made actual in bread and wine. The gestures, the words will be repeated, but the reality will persist unchanged: the sacrificial offering of the body and blood of Christ made once and for all. Because blood is life (Lv 17:11) and flow of blood makes one live, Jesus' blood symbolizes and effects a forceful union between God and his people.

The sense of the uniqueness of the Lord's Supper has from the earliest times characterized the Catholic tradition. Beginning with St. Paul, the stream of Christian conviction gradually clarified itself into the statement that the Eucharist is a sacramental sacrifice of communion with God. Of this development it may be said that Eucharistic teaching developed parallel with the nascent Christology of the Church; as in its origin so in its further explication, the evaluation of the Eucharist was based on the estimate of the Person of the Lord who instituted it.

Paul's Eucharistic language is markedly realistic and finds no parallel in the language used about other sacraments. The Eucharist, like the manna, is spiritual, supernatural food (1 Cor 10:3-4). It brings participation in the body and blood of Christ, and so maintains the unity of the Church (1 Cor 10:16-17). It is a feast upon the Lord's sacrifice analogous to the sacrificial feasts both of Jews and Gentiles (1 Cor 10:18-22). St. Paul thinks of Christ as the true Paschal victim (1 Cor 5:7). The Eucharist is a real identification with Christ as sacrificed and through sacrifice glorified, and not a merely symbolic identification, one which we require for our preservation and growth as men re-created in him; and there is no better way of saying that the Lord gives what we need than to say that the body which was for us on the Cross, and is for us still (1 Cor 11:24), is given to be our food; and the blood, which has ratified the new covenant, to be our drink. In the physical world the fullest identification that we know, is that of food and drink with the bodies which depend upon them for their support and growth. All of Paul's teaching on the Eucharist grows out of thoughts of the Passover and the covenant feast of Ex 24:1-11, immeasurably deepened and spiritualized by that doctrine of the union of Christ with his people, which St. Paul had received from Christ himself (Ac 9:5).

There is in the Eucharist a communication of life, but there is nothing magical about it. It rests upon the divine appointment but it requires the cooperation of our faith. Perhaps we may find in Ph 3:10-14 the best description provided by St. Paul of the right dispositions. Faith is essentially practical and only attains its full reality in the action to which it leads. Sacraments both at the beginning of the Christian life and throughout its course give to faith opportunities for its exercise and so maintain both its reality and its simplicity. When the sacraments are neglected, faith too remains in the air, or loses itself in a maze of auto-suggestion.

8.

THE EUCHARIST IN MARK AND MATTHEW

The Marcan, the earliest of the Synoptic accounts of the institution of the Eucharist (Mk 14:22-25), represents a liturgical formulation of what happened at the Last Supper. Its vocabulary and style suggest that it comes from a Jerusalem or Palestinian liturgy. As in the earliest Eucharist anaphorae, the account of the institution of the rite was recited to give authority to the repetition of the rite. Mark's concern is not simply to relate what Jesus did and said on that occasion, but to recount it in the interest of Christian faith and worship. Hence the reader is introduced in medias res. Mt 26:26-29 is close to Mark's text.

Mark's account of the institution of the Lord's Supper is concise almost to the point of obscurity, but it brings before us the second main line of teaching in his gospel concerning the work of Christ. Mk 10:45 and 14:24 indicate these two main lines of the teaching of Mark's gospel. Our Lord's life, laid down sacrificially, is a "ransom for many" and "the blood of the covenant." The former effects deliverance from sin and judgment, while the latter provides covenant relationship and fellowship between God and men.

It is important to understand the significance of the Supper, which has been observed ever since as the central act of Christian worship. The Marcan narrative reveals the singularly original manner in which Jesus conceived the nature of his redemptive death and related

THE EUCHARIST

the Eucharist thereto. The words of institution are given in their simplest form, but are eloquent in their very simplicity. The Supper is at once an anticipation of the Messianic feast (Mk 14:25) and a bond of union, a covenant (24); the note of sacrifice is present in the Passover associations of the meal, and is explicitly brought out in the phrase "poured out for many" (24). This last time that he would touch wine before his death, Jesus consecrated it to a special relationship, to the blood he was about to shed. The new covenant of Jeremiah's prophecy (31:31-34) is about to be inaugurated "by the blood of a better sacrifice" (Heb 8:10).

"As they were eating he took some bread, and when he had said the blessing he broke it and gave it to them. Take it, he said, this is my body" (Mk 14:22). The blessing was an act of thanksgiving to God and probably took the normal Jewish form. The words, "This is my body" are the same in all four New Testament accounts with a slight inversion in St. Paul. The phrase probably became ritually fixed before the writing of the gospels. Jn 6:51 suggests the language that might actually have been used by our Lord: "The bread that I shall give is my flesh, for the life of the world."

Mark never puts into our Lord's mouth such figurative expressions as "I am the door," or the like, and there is no reason at all to suppose that he and his readers did not understand the language of our Lord at the institution to mean just what it said. The words are so familiar that it is impossible for us to realize how the tremendous claim here made must have startled any outsider, however much in sympathy with the Christian ideal, into whose hands the gospel may have come. "Take" indicates that Christ's death with its benefits was a gift which his disciples must appropriate, and that this appropriation is of a most intimate kind comparable with the assimilation of food, and a partaking of its nourishment and efficacy.

The purpose of any such sacred meal was to initiate those who partook, into more intimate union with God. This was the purpose of all the sacrificial meals of the Old Testament. In this case the eating of Christ's body and especially the drinking of his blood, are obvious means of union to God through Christ. This is particularly clear of the blood, for the Jews were forbidden to partake of the blood of any victim; it represented the life itself, and as such belonged to God. Partaking of the blood of Jesus means sharing his God-given life. The Eucharist interpreted as food, as bread and wine, is clearly meant as the source of new life for men.

"Then he took a cup, and when he had returned thanks, he gave it to them, and all drank from it, and he said to them, This is my blood, the blood of the covenant, which is to be poured out for many" (23-24). Jesus interprets the cup of wine in terms of covenant blood, an allusion to the sacrifice that concluded the Sinai covenant (Ex 24:8, Zc 9:11, Heb 9:15-22). Underlying the identification he makes, is the meaning of blood as the life of the victim (Lv 17:11, 14). The blessings for Israel implied in the poured out blood of the Sinai covenant are now seen as a type of the blessings to come to all men in the poured out life of Jesus. As at Sinai Moses sealed the covenant of Yahweh with his people with the blood of the victims, so on the cross Jesus the perfect victim is about to seal with his own blood, the new covenant between God and man foretold by the prophets (Jr 31:31-34). Jesus takes on himself the task of universal redemption that Isaiah assigns to the servant of Yahweh (Is 42:6, 49:6, 53:12). In the background of Jesus' words are several important ideas of Jewish religion: man's sins lead to death; God has rescued his people, as from Egypt, and may be trusted to deliver from death itself; God forgives men in mercy, if they obey him; God will make a new covenant.

To a Jew the blood of the covenant meant the blood by which the old covenant was ratified and Israel constituted God's people, but there was also in the background the older rite of the blood of circumcision by which individuals were incorporated into this chosen people (Gn 17:10). As the blood of the ratification of the old covenant was distributed to its members by sprinkling, so also the blood which ratifies the new covenant. The rite, therefore, both constitutes the new, covenanted people of God, and incorporates into this people those who participate in it.

"Poured out for many" should be understood in the Semitic sense as designating a great number without restriction, the multitude. It really means all. The thought of Jesus' coming sacrifice is ever in the background of Mark's text. It is gently alluded to by the phrase "poured out for many for the forgiveness of sins." This recalls the prophecy of Is 53:11-12, of the atonement for Israel to be effected by the servant of the Lord. This prophecy was prominent in the thought, not only of the early Church, but of Jesus himself in his reflection upon his imminent suffering. At this solemn moment he thus interprets the coming Passion. The Last Supper, at which, according to John 17, Jesus consecrated himself for his imminent death at the hand of others, is the one occasion in the Synoptic gospels where Jesus gives his death a sacrificial interpretation.

"I tell you solemnly, I shall not drink any more wine until I drink the new wine in the kingdom of God" (25). This is an allusion to the eschatological banquet; Jesus and his disciples will never meet at table again. This saying rejoins the allusion of Paul (1 Cor 11:26) and shows that the Eucharist was celebrated by the early

Christians in joyful expectation of the final coming of
Christ and the definitive establishment of the kingdom
of the Father, in which all things will be renewed (Rv
21:1-5). Jesus declares once again that he will soon die,
but he does so in a Eucharistic and eschatological way
which will be clarified by Luke (22:16). He looks forward
beyond his death to his risen life and to the perfect fellowship of the consummated kingdom. The table of the
Lord has a forward aspect towards the consummation of
Christ's work, as well as a backward reference to the
Cross. The First Supper looked forward to the Cross, all
others look back to it as well as forward to the Parousia.
The Eucharist will be for Christ and for us a festival of
reunion and victory, until he comes again in glory.

Mt 26:26-29 follows Mark closely, but in his characteristic way, he explains the meaning of Mark's "take" by
adding "eat"; he makes it clear that the drinking of the
cup was in response to a definitive command to do so,
and adds "for the forgiveness of sins." All these additions
are valuable and may have been found in the consecration prayer to which Matthew was accustomed. "Now as
they were eating, Jesus took some bread and when he
had said the blessing, he broke it and gave it to the disciples. Take it and eat it, he said, this is my body" (26).
As in Mark, the taking of bread and the drinking of the
cup are described as occurring during the course of a
meal, rather than as a separate ceremony. In all likelihood this was the way the earliest Church celebrated the
Supper until excesses at the common meal required that
the meal and the Eucharist be separated (1 Cor 11:20-21).

"Then he took a cup, and when he had returned thanks
he gave it to them. Drink all of you from this, he said, for
this is my blood, the blood of the covenant, which is to
be poured out for many for the forgiveness of sins" (27-
28). The bread symbolizes Jesus' total self which is given
for man; the cup symbolizes the life of Jesus which is

offered up to seal the new covenant by which God is calling into being his new people, the Church. Only Matthew
adds the phrase that expresses more clearly the effect of
Christ's reconciling death. Certain Israelite sacrifices
atoned for sin and guilt, by which were meant ritual
offenses. The atoning death of Jesus liberates man not
only from ritual sin and guilt, but from sin simply, for
which there was no atonement in the Israelite sacrificial
system. Our Lord's language is throughout anticipatory,
as his blood had not yet been poured out. He gave himself with his own hand by anticipation and deliberate
will, but not yet as he would give himself after his glorification (Jn 6:62-63). As yet his flesh and blood were not
glorified, nor had the faith of the Apostles reached the
stage at which they could fully assimilate such food. The
Lord's words speak of his body and blood as a sacrifice
to God and as the means of a sacrificial feast. It is by
partaking of the latter that we claim in faith the pardon
and new life won by the former.

Mark 1:4 gives the detail "for the forgiveness of sins,"
as the teaching of John the Baptist: "a baptism of repentance for the forgiveness of sins." By introducing it here,
Matthew echoes the prophecy of Jeremias, about the new
covenant, and emphasizes the thought of sacrifice: "I will
forgive their iniquity and never call their sins to mind"
(Jr 31:34). Matthew alone omits this phrase in reference
to John's baptism in 3:2; it looks as if he wishes to emphasize that the true basis of forgiveness is the redeeming
death of Christ.

"From now on, I tell you, I shall not drink wine until
the day I drink the new wine with you in the kingdom
of my Father" (29). The immediate point is that this is
the Lord's last meal on earth. The first Communion opens
the perspective of the eternal communion in the Father's
house. The Lord's Supper is a type and prophecy of the
eternal marriage supper of the Lamb (Rv 19:9). The

Supper looks forward to the Messianic banquet as well
as backward to the mighty act of redemption. New wine
is wine of a higher order, the heavenly joy of which
earthly wine is a symbol. Newness is a frequent Messianic theme.

The theological and apologetic importance of the Last
Supper needs to be underlined. On the night of the Last
Supper the fortunes of Jesus were at their lowest ebb.
There was treason in his own camp. The triumph of his
enemies was at hand, and he looked forward with cer-
tainty on the morrow to the degrading death of a common malefactor. Yet he chose this moment to ordain a
rite in which his death should be commemorated by his
followers to the end of time, showing that he foresaw
his resurrection and the future triumph of his cause. Such
conduct under such circumstances shows a strictly supernatural gift of faith and insight. Moreover he chose this
moment of deepest depression and seeming failure, for
the most studied declaration of his true divinity. For what
less than divine can he be said to be, whose death atones
for the sins of the whole world, and reconciles the human
race to God? And how can he be other than the author
of life himself, who declares that his body and blood are
the spiritual food and drink of mankind?

The Lord's Supper is not a bare commemoration of the
Lord's death; Christians in all ages have believed that
attached to devout and reverent participation in the Eucharistic rite, is a special covenant blessing which ordin-
arily cannot be obtained in any other way, and which is
necessary for the nourishment and growth of the spiritual life. Such a view seems clearly to underlie the statement of Paul (1 Cor 10:16) about the cup of blessing.

The covenanted blessing is generally conceived as a
special realization of the union between the believer and
his Savior, as suggested by our Lord's own allegory of
the vine and the branches (Jn 15) spoken immediately

after the institution, and by that of the Bread of Life
(Jn 6) which was intended to prepare the way for it. It
is especially true at the table of the Eucharist that "Christ
dwells in our hearts by faith," "we are one with Christ
and Christ with us," "we dwell in him and he in us," and
he is in us the fountain of life, sanctification, and cleansing.

The primary reference of the rite is to the death of
Christ. The body given for us, the blood poured out symbolize the atoning death upon the cross. It is implied that
those who with faith and due thankfulness approach the
table, obtain remission of their sins and all other benefits
of Christ's passion. At the same time, the reference is not
exclusively to Christ's death. He does not say, "Do this
in remembrance of my death," but in remembrance of
me, that is, of all that I am to Christians: of my incarnation, resurrection, and ascension, as well as of my death.
To the early Christians the rite was largely a memorial
of the Resurrection and as such was regularly celebrated
on the first day of the week (Ac 20:7). Accordingly in the
Supper it is with the ascended Lord that the Christians
hold communion. While commemorating the tragedy of
Calvary, he communes with him who is alive for ever
and ever (Rv 1:18). He joins in the heavenly worship of
the Lamb who still bears the marks of his slaughter (Rv
5:6) and who in recompense for his humiliation is now
endowed with almighty power.

Christ is present in the Eucharist not only in his deity
but also in his glorified humanity and in some spiritual
and ineffable, but still most real manner, and imparts to
believers his godhead by making us partakers of his sacred body and blood. We are here in the presence of very
deep mysteries of which we should speak with awe and
reverence, remembering how very limited our faculties
are.

Finally, the Lord's Supper is a memorial rite. "Do this

in remembrance of me," as my memorial (Lk 22:19, 1 Cor
11:24). This is especially a memorial before man, a recall
of the highlights of salvation history, but it is also a
pleading before God, the Father, of the merits of the
precious death of his Son (Heb 7:24).

9.

THE SACRAMENTS IN JOHN'S GOSPEL

The Church, an important theme in John's Gospel, is inseparable from the sacraments. The works of Christ that the Spirit perpetuates are chiefly the Church and the sacraments. The liturgical and sacramental character of the fourth Gospel is more and more recognized today.

Many of the Johannine discourses of Jesus undoubtedly refer directly to the sacraments or have them as a background. The conversation with Nicodemus (Jn 3:1-21) refers to Baptism. John tells us that through baptismal water God begets children unto himself and pours forth upon them his Spirit: "Unless a man is born through water and the Spirit, he cannot enter the kingdom of God" (3:5). Thus Baptism becomes a source of eternal life: "the water that I shall give will turn into a spring welling up to eternal life" (4:14). Baptism is assumed as well known to the readers, as the Eucharist is assumed in chapter 6.

The discourse on the bread of life (ch. 6) ultimately (6:51-58) refers to the Eucharist. Jesus is the true bread both as the word of God's revelation (32-33) and as the victim offered in sacrifice by his body and blood given for the life of the world (51-58). "The bread that I shall give is my flesh for the life of the world" (51). The word flesh suggests a relation between the Eucharist and the Incarnation: man is nourished by the Word made flesh. The Eucharist is an indispensable means of transmitting God's life to men through Jesus: "As I who am sent by the

living Father myself draw life from the Father, so whoever eats me draws life from me" (57). The believer's life
is intimately bound up with Christ's. The life that the
Father communicates to his Son passes to the faithful
through the Eucharist. To live is to enter in communion
with the Son and through him with the Father; this exchange consists in mutual knowledge and love, and is
offered as something stable and definitive. The Eucharistic meal is the privileged moment of this communion
which has in itself the secret of everlasting life.

Even granting that Jn 6:51-58 might be an addition,
the fact remains that there are already cultic and sacramental elements in chapter 6, even without these verses
which just make the Evangelist's thought more explicit.
As in the Cana scene (ch. 2) and in the description of
the true vine (ch. 15), in a symbolic way John suggests
that the Eucharistic wine means a new dispensation replacing the old, and that the Eucharistic bread is the real
bread from heaven replacing the manna: "It is my Father
who gives you the bread from heaven, the true bread"
(6:32).

Some of our Lord's miracles in John are symbolic of
the sacraments by which the glorified Christ sanctifies
souls in the Church. It would seem that the miracle at
the wedding at Cana (Jn 2:1-11) includes some Eucharistic symbolism. The wine is clearly Jesus' gift of salvation for which light, water, and food are other Johannine
symbols. The miracle, however, has also some secondary
Eucharistic overtones which some Fathers see even in
the mention of choice wine (10). The hour of Jesus which
formally begins at the Last Supper (13:1) has not yet
come (2:4). The Passover dating here (2:13), as in the
multiplication of the loaves (6:5), might suggest some
vague relation or anticipation of the Eucharistic bread
and wine, the Christian Passover. The wine and wedding
could also be a distant symbolic reference to the Eucha-

rist, the sacramental wine that refreshes man's soul and is the center of the liturgical life of the Church. The miracle also falls in with John's constant purpose of pointing out the inadequacy of Jewish ritual cleansing; water brought for that purpose (2:6) is changed into something richer and more gladdening, into wine which at the Last Supper was used for the Eucharist, the wine of the Spirit (Ep 5:18). Judaism is water, Christianity is wine; and it is Christ who makes all the difference.

Christ significantly began his public life with a miracle of **transformation**: his whole mission was to convert sinners into saints, to turn darkness into light, grief into joy, to make death the gate of life, to elevate earth to heaven. The miracle of Cana was, moreover, a miracle of festive joy and gladness, of more than royal munificence, showing how the Gospel is a religion of true happiness. Christ relieves not only the present need but also provides for the future; the miracle has also a representative value. Its essential character is to be a sign of sovereign power; it manifests Christ as Lord of matter as well as of the spirit. He has power over the elements of bread and wine as shown by the multiplication of the loaves and the changing of the water into wine; he also has power over his own body as shown by his walking on the water (Jn 6:16-21). Considering its circumstantial character, the miracle is the change of the simple to the richer element. In its moral character it is the answer of love to faith, ministering to the fullness of human joy in one of its simplest and most natural forms. For us today the lesson is not only that we must be transformed by Christ's power but that it must happen not in a spirit of gloomy religiosity but in the context of joyous human fellowship. The transposition or application of these notions as a remote preparation to the Eucharist is easy and natural. What happened in that home at Cana should happen in our souls; it should lead us to larger spiritual truth, as it led the witnesses of the miracle, and this is realized in a special way through the Eucharist.

The multiplication of the loaves (Jn 6:1-15) holds a central place in all four Gospels. It indicates the summit and the end of the Galilean ministry, and the moment of the decisive option between faith in and rejection of Jesus. All the accounts of the multiplication have a strong Eucharistic motif. As the event was handed down in the teaching tradition of the Christian community, its connection with the special food of God's people, the Eucharist, was recognized. There is a close parallel in gesture and word with the Synoptic descriptions of the Last Supper: "He took the loaves, gave thanks, and gave them out to all" (Jn 6:11). It would then seem that the wording of the multiplication accounts was colored by the Eucharistic liturgies familiar to the various communities. That all traditions would have this Eucharistic coloring means that the insight into the relationship of the multiplication of the loaves and the action of the Last Supper must have been gained early in the Christian preaching tradition.

The miracle leads up to the discourse that follows and it illustrates the Eucharist. It is a pendant to chapter 3, emphasizing the presence of the Spirit as carrying on in the Eucharist the life given in Baptism; to chapter 4 showing Jesus' power to give spiritual nourishment; to chapter 5 in the reassertion of his claims in spite of controversy. It is also a further instance of Christ's insight into men's hearts (6:15, 26, 61, 2:21). There is also a striking analogy to the incident in Elisha's life (2 K 4:42-44) which may have been in the Evangelist's mind (Christ is a prophet, and far more than Elisha) and also to God's feeding of the Israelites in the wilderness (Ps 78:23-25).

As with all the signs in John's Gospel, the feeding of the multitude points to the denouement in Jesus' death and resurrection. The incident is dated at Passover (6:4). Jesus' thanks over the food (11) is expressed by the verbal form of "thanksgiving" or "Eucharist" which by the time the Gospel was written had probably already become a common term for the commemoration of Jesus' Last Supper. The miraculous crossing of the sea that follows (Jn 6:16-24), the discourse on the living bread from heaven (25-58), and the subtle reference to Jesus' ascension and the gift of the Spirit (60-63) and many other allusions suggest the new redemptive Exodus. The confession of Peter (68-69, Mk 8:27-30) anticipates the confession of the Church, as of all true believers, in the "Holy one of God."

The miracle illustrates the mode of Christ's working in all ages; both in temporal and spiritual things, the spirit that proceeds from him makes the greatest results possible to the smallest means; that which appears, as to quantity, most trifling, multiplies itself by his divine power, so as to supply the wants of thousands. The physical miracle is for us a type of the spiritual one which his words work in the life of mankind in all time. The miracle illustrates in particular the Lord's power to feed the spiritual needs of the masses with his teaching (Am 8:11; Jn 6:21-50) and with the Eucharistic food (51-58).

The miracle teaches Christ's creative power and lordship over nature; his benevolence and bounty giving his people enough and more than enough. It suggests that he can give the spiritual food of mankind, the bread of life, sustaining the souls of those who believe in him. In particular, the miracle is a figure of the Lord's Supper, in which, through the agency of his ministers, he feeds the multitudes with the spiritual food of his most precious body and blood. Christ indeed is the Bread of the world, the unexhausted and unexhaustible source of all life for the spiritual needs of hungering souls in all ages.

The miracles of Jesus drew attention to his wondrous personality and all-sufficing Gospel. For of all miracles he is the greatest.

The crowds drew a wrong conclusion and looked on Jesus as a Bread-King (Jn 6:15), who would supply their needs without any labor on their part. Jesus drew the right conclusion by describing himself as the true Bread of God. The next day this miracle became the basis of the great testing-discourse, delivered to many of the same people in the synagogue at Capernaum, upon himself as the Bread of Life, the Bread of God come down from heaven to give life to the world.

There is more here than the mere multiplication of bread. This meal has Messianic significance. It was a sort of Galilean Lord's Supper. Once Jesus told a parable about a great supper which symbolized the kingdom of God (Lk 14:15-24) and for which the invitation went out, "Come for all things are now ready." Now Jesus acts out the parable, so that the bread becomes the Bread of the kingdom or in John's idiom the Bread of Life.

The miracle of the loaves was remembered and valued as a type of the Christian Eucharist. This suggests that the event had a quasi-sacramental character; the meal was important for its meaning as well as for the physical nourishment of the people. The first Christians saw it as related to the teaching of Jesus on the coming kingdom and so regarded it also as an anticipation of the eschatological banquet. John's discourse on the Bread of Life contains eschatological themes which he handles in characteristic style, and it is probable that he regarded both the feeding and the Eucharist in this light.

Baptism and the Eucharist are suggested in Jn 19:34: "One of the soldiers pierced his side with a lance; and immediately there came out blood and water." According to rabbinical tradition man's body is composed of water and blood; the effusion of these two elements would then indicate the reality of Christ's death. John considers this fact symbolically. The life of Jesus, now closed on earth, continues to be imparted and to flow into the life of his followers in his Spirit-empowered gifts of Baptism and Eucharist, or what the ancient Church significantly called the Paschal mystery.

The sacraments draw their efficacy from the sacrificial death of Christ. Jesus Christ is Savior not simply by having been declared the Messiah at the time of his baptism (through water) but by having fulfilled his mission in his death on the cross (through blood). Consequently, as the object of faith he must be confessed as one who has come "not in water only but in the water and the blood" (1 Jn 5:6). John customarily writes on several levels, making his narrative of historical events significant to his readers in respect to the enduring Christian realities. "Water and blood" also means the continuing witness given in the Church through the Spirit especially in the sacraments of Baptism and the Eucharist. "Therefore there are three who testify, the Spirit and the water and the blood and the three are one" (1 Jn 5:7). The three support each other; the water of Baptism is accompanied by the Spirit and the Spirit came through the blood of the death of Jesus. The baptismal water and the Eucharistic blood have the source of their existence and power in the death of Jesus and the intervention of the Holy Spirit. By saying that there are three witnesses in favor of Jesus, John is saying that God has sufficiently accredited his Son before men, as satisfying the legal requirements of the Old Testament law (Dt 19:15).

Finally, in view of St. John's sacramental interest the fact that he does not record the institution of the Lord's Supper is surprising. However, what needed to be said on this score had already been said in chapter 6; in fact, verse 51, "The bread that I shall give is my flesh for the life of the world" can easily be seen as the Johannine form of the words of institution. Actually, the Synoptic tradition identifies the last meal of Jesus with the Jewish Passover and practically reduces the account of the Last Supper to the Eucharistic words of institution which may be used at any meal where bread and wine are blessed. John (chs. 13-17) stresses the correlation of the slaying of the Paschal Lamb with Jesus' death and explains the practical meaning and consequences of what happened at the Last Supper. He concentrates on the theme of discipleship and passes over the Eucharistic words which for him were the basis for a very different development. As Jn 6:51 shows, John values the Eucharistic words as a means of inculcating his very important theme of the necessity of the passion. As he had already treated this theme sufficiently in different ways throughout chapters 7-12, he did not need to treat it afresh in his account of the Last Supper. In fact, he chose to use the supper traditions as the starting-point for extended treatment of another important theme, the meaning of discipleship and of Christian love. Because it unfolds the meaning of the Eucharist, he emphasizes the washing of the feet which the other Evangelists had missed. It is so much easier to worship a word than to follow a deed. The words "This is my body" are well enshrined in our Eucharistic services but the test of our partaking of Christ's body is his spirit manifested in our lives.

What a comparison with the Synoptics does show is how John treats of Baptism and the Eucharist without associating these sacraments with any single all-important saying of Jesus considered as part of his departing instructions to his disciples. The Johannine references to these sacraments are scattered in scenes throughout the ministry of Jesus. This fits in with the Gospel's intention of showing how the institutions of our Christian life are rooted in what Jesus said and did in his life. Among the four Gospels it is to John most of all that we owe the deep Christian understanding of Baptism and the Eucharist. John used symbolism because it is only through symbolism that he could teach his sacramental theology and still remain faithful to the literary form of his Gospel. In so doing he showed the sacramental undertones of the words and works of Jesus that were already part of the Gospel tradition.

10.

THIS IS MY BODY

These simple words are no doubt the most important that were ever spoken by Jesus, words that are repeated throughout the centuries all over the world, and take on particular meaning according to who pronounces them: Jesus at the Last Supper, the priest at the altar, every believer at the crossroads of his life.

When Jesus said, "This is my body," he summarized orally and ritually the whole mystery of his human life. He recalled his coming in the flesh in Mary's womb; he anticipated his death by adding "given for you"; he announced his resurrection by which he would be able to continue the gift of himself that he was announcing; in one word he instituted the holy Eucharist.

Truly incarnated, the Son of God has assumed a specific human nature and our human condition; not an ideal humanity but a "sinful body" (Rm 8:3) with its limits, helplessness, fragilities. Paul even says that for our sakes God made Christ to be sin (2 Cor 5:21) though not a sinner. The sinless Christ bore the burden of our sins, that we might be acquitted. He experienced everything human but sin (Heb 4:15). The Last Supper is the ritual celebration of our redemption, our Passover from sin to grace. To be ours, to be eaten, to become our bread, a body of grace, Christ's body must become a body of glory, a risen body. The Passion is the preparation of the bread, to make it edible "for us and for the multitude," for the whole human race. The Eucharist has in the form

of a meal, the contents of Calvary to be applied to the
faithful whenever the need arises, that is, constantly during all the succeeding ages. "This is my body" is said by
Christ both to his Father and to us. Christ's sacrifice
offered to the Father in the Eucharist is also constantly
made available to all men. Our acceptance of Christ's
body demands our recognition of his work of salvation,
"the recognizing of the body of the Lord" (1 Cor 11:29),
the body of sin, but also the body of glory and of grace.
Christ's Passion cannot be forgotten; it has a living
memorial in the total victory of the Resurrection, and
in the Eucharist, the bread baked at the fire of Christ's
sufferings. Easter is not the end of the redemptive Incarnation but its glorification. Christ's body is now the
glorified risen body of Jesus of Nazareth who is now
Christ, the Lord (Ac 2:26), whom Stephen saw at the
right of the Father (Ac 7:55), and who is able to give
himself to his Church as he promised he would, once he
had ascended "to where he was before" (Jn 6:62). All that
Jesus said about the bread of life must be viewed in the
light of two facts, the glorious Ascension and the gift of
the Spirit. His return to heaven is a proof of his coming
from heaven. The whole process of the return of Christ
to the glory of the Father, including as it did the crucifixion, was both the supreme scandal and the vindication
of Christ as the bread of life. All power and authority
in heaven and on earth has now been given to the risen
Christ (Mt 28:18), and he wants to give himself to his
Church, his mystical body, as a body of grace, a source
of salvation. This he does through the Holy Spirit: "It is
the spirit who gives life" (Jn 6:62). It is by the Spirit that
Christ rose to life (Ac 1:2) and it is the Spirit who gives
life to the Church (Ac 1:4). The Church makes the Eucharist, in which she contemplates the mystery of her own
life in the Spirit, when she obeys Christ's command and
repeats the Last Supper as he demanded, "Do this in

memory of me." But inversely it is also the Eucharist that makes the Church by the gift of Christ's body of grace. And to eat the body of Christ is to receive his whole body, it is to become members of one another. Such is some of the meaning of the phrase, "This is my body," on the lips of Jesus.

On the lips of the priest the Eucharistic words, "This is my body," suppose a certain identification of Christ with his minister who is not simply quoting but speaking in the name of Christ. That is why the Eucharist is a prayer that is always heard. Its language is not empty but an actual performance, like the word of God which does what it says. The Eucharistic action has the power to make present the risen Lord, as he is in glory always interceding in our behalf (Rm 8:34), in the consummation of his historical work of reconciliation. The words of the priest are repeated because he acts as a minister, not as a vice-redeemer. Christ's offering at Mass is actual but not new. The newness is on the part of the Church, the mystical body which grows with each celebration. The Eucharist shows the role of the priest and the power of his word as God's minister. His role is to represent Christ, as head of the body which is the Church, to strengthen his brothers in their faith (Lk 22:32). God's word entrusted to him, assimilated in prayer, and expressed in his preaching, appears in the consecration at Mass as it really is, productive in building up the body of Christ.

When Jesus said, "Do this in memory of me" he meant directly that what he did at the Last Supper should be repeated at the Eucharistic celebration, but he also was asking every Christian to offer his own body as a holy sacrifice truly pleasing to God (Rm 12:1). Each one of us must pronounce in our own existence, in our service of God, a true, "This is my body." Looking at the consecrated Host each Christian should be able to say, "this is my body," since Jesus present in the Host is the true

man, the new Adam (Ep 2:15), the prototype of the new
humanity that God has created in his person. The sacrament of the altar contains three realities that some find
difficulty in reconciling: adoration, fraternity, and eschatology. Yet the Eucharistic body of Christ reminds us
that our body comes from a Father-Creator, and that it
must be dedicated to him in a filial spirit. It tells us that
our body is related to that of the Son of God who was
incarnated to enter into communion with the human family and ultimately make it part of God's family. It also
promises to associate our body one day to the glorious
resurrection of Christ's body. "Become what you receive,"
said St. Augustine. If there is repetition of the Eucharist,
it is because our efforts must constantly be renewed. The
Eucharist is a sign which demands a countersign, the
laying of our own lives on the altar with Christ's own
sacrifice. Our lives will then be a Holy Thursday night,
that is, the eve of the Passion but also the preparation for
Easter-Pentecost.

All this supposes that Christ's body is really "given
to us" in the Eucharist. Granted that Eucharistic piety
may have exaggerated in the past its approach to the
real presence of Christ in the Eucharist, that is no reason
to consider this divine presence in a purely subjective
way, the way for example that the donor is part of his
gift. It is not enough to consider the Eucharist as so much
blessed bread. On the contrary, to really appreciate the
personal presence of Christ in the Eucharist, the Eucharistic bread must be digested spiritually in pious contemplation, with a faith which opens wide especially the
eyes of the heart, but also sees the advantage of exposing
to our bodily eyes such a meaningful sign as the consecrated Host.

The presence of Christ in the Eucharist is the presence
of a risen body, of a complete Person, not of a separated
soul, nor of an idea, or a simple souvenir. It is a presence

that has no parallel and consequently is hard to specify in so many words. To qualify it as spiritual or mystical is true but insufficient. It is sometimes described as physical, in the sense of real, but the term physical normally refers to the domain of our sense, and real again is general since it applies also to all the other presences of Christ to his Church. To call it a bodily presence is true but again misleading because we have not as yet any experience of a risen body. Sacramental is another good adjective but it is also true of all the sacraments which are all encounters with Christ. But there is a difference between Christ's presence in the Eucharist and in the other sacraments. There as here he is present as an efficacious sign, but the other sacraments are signs of his action, whereas the Eucharist is also the sign of his personal presence as our bread of life. The altar is not the house of Nazareth and the Eucharist is not a continuation of Christ's earthly life. Yet it is not a matter of indifference that a sign is given, a sign that comprises a physical localization; the sacrament is here and not elsewhere. It implies a precise focus in space and time as the human reference to the mystery. It would then be to depreciate the mystery, if one were to refuse to go where the sacrament is celebrated or reserved, on the pretext that God can be loved and worshiped anywhere. The new liturgy has not committed this error since it recommends that the Blessed Sacrament be reserved in a prominent and easily available part of the Church, where the faithful may come for quiet prayer and meditation before the Eucharist.

The real presence of Christ in the Eucharist is meant as our bread to be consumed in order to realize the unity of the Church. The Eucharist is not a spectacle with transubstantiation as the key attraction; it is a sacrificial meal. Not a meal that is rushed but a banquet that is carefully prepared and thoroughly appreciated. One in which provision is made for the absent, one that is never finished. Jesus remains present as long as the species last, according to the mind and ordinance of the Church. One communion prepares the next one. The reserved sacrament invites us to prayerful appreciation of God's gift of his Son. The custom of visualizing the Eucharist by solemn exposition has surely much good traditional thinking in its favor, when it is done tastefully and soberly. To think otherwise would be the manifestation of an allergy to aesthetics and a propensity to the utilitarian. The connoisseur enjoys the flicker of good wine in his glass before sipping it; is it not at the same time something beautiful as well as something good? To eliminate the visual appreciation of food at a banquet, or converse with the guests and especially the host, would be to drop our jaws into our plate and reduce the act of eating to the level of bestial gorging. If we expose the sacred Host for all to see it is because we are proud to flaunt an expressive sign.

Furthermore, eating our Lord's body is ordained to the fostering of the Trinitarian life in our soul. In holy Communion Christ performs his role of mediator, leading us to the Father through the Holy Spirit. Communion is not a blind alley, a dead-end leading to Jesus; it is rather the introduction to the intimate mystery of God by him "in whose body lives the fullness of divinity" (Col 2:9). The reception of holy Communion and prayer before the Blessed Sacrament both have the same object and the same purpose. Adoration prolongs our meal and allows time for assimilation, digestion. To take time to venerate the Eucharist is to offer oneself to union with God which cannot be achieved at the bat of an eye; it is to understand that the symbolism of this food is the union of persons. We do not love Christ like the wolf who devours his prey, the lamb. Human tenderness involves beaming contemplation. By neglecting adoration, the celebration itself would soon become banal, spiritless, and holy Communion would lose its appeal.

The Eucharist will give us strength and encourage us in the struggle of life, but we must first experience Christ's love personally before we seek to use it in our practical life. Holy Communion demands the unconditional surrender of our life to God, our submission to the gentle mastery of Christ, to his demanding but rewarding claims, the liberation of his yoke (Mt 11:28-30). But a transfusion of moral character is not done in a minute. We must take time to prostrate ourselves in the presence of the Eucharist. To do so is not to use the Eucharist as a pretext for loafing on the job instead of working at the Christian apostolate. Communion is the reception of our working orders from the Spirit himself, so that the building of Christ's body may proceed according to plan. To take the time to adore is to bring back to the altar our fatigue, the burdens of our days, our joys and our anxieties. Unless we take the necessary time out for prayer, our work will compete with our contemplation, our projects will lack a spiritual dimension, the poor will compete with Christ in our spiritual life, our difficulties will end up in bitterness and discouragement. The only lasting apostolic work is the one which finds its support in the Holy Eucharist; anything less is not only essentially limited but lacks its proper inspiration and affords only problematic successes. It is as difficult to adore silently before the Blessed Sacrament, as it is to take time to receive and listen to our brother, and both are inseparably bound together. To adore is to assimilate all the kindness of which we are the object on the part of God, in order to share it with our neighbor. The first Christians had well understood that the breaking of the bread is a contagious gesture which inspires many other forms of sharing (Ac 2:42-47). The Lord's Supper is in-

separable from the washing of our brothers' feet (Jn
13:1-15). Without our presence both to the needs of our
brothers and to the claims of our Master in prayer, the
Eucharistic feast would not be the Lord's Supper (1 Cor
11:20) but a meaningless comedy, like a cocktail party
with all its frivolity, superficiality, and inconsequence.

11.

DO THIS IN MEMORY OF ME

"Eat and drink the Eucharistic bread and wine in memory of me." Our Lord's command brings together God, man, and the world; in it love and obedience coincide, action and contemplation are united; in the Eucharist Christian ethics, that is, moral action, motivation, and character find their source and their purpose.

Man must eat to live; there is a natural, biological relation between food and human growth. But revelation goes further by indicating a food which is more substantial than material bread. "Man does not live by bread alone, but on every word that comes from the mouth of God." This is a quote from Dt 8:3 which states that God makes all things by his word, and so gives life to Israel by means of the commandments that issue from his mouth. The Israelites are urged to abandon themselves to the providence of God who can sustain them if necessary, as history shows, with manna in place of bread. From the discipline of hunger and the discovery of manna, Israel learnt that man lives by everything that comes out of God's mouth, that is, his commands and words which convey all the benefits of life, material, physical, spiritual. Man is utterly dependent on God for guidance, nourishment, raiment, health, and spiritual education. Material sustenance no less than spiritual comes from God and it is not sufficient of itself. Man depends on God for everything.

In Dt 6:11 "to eat and be full" is proposed without

further discussion as a blessing from God. This is repeated in 8:10: in the promised land "you will eat and have all you want and you will bless Yahweh in the rich land he has given you." But such is the heart of man that in the midst of gifts he can forget the giver. The manna is a proof that ultimately man is sustained by the creative word of God. It is this word which brings bread, manna, or any other sustenance into existence, and therefore it is this word which gives life. The implications are clear: not only should the abundance of Palestine be attributed to God's word, but if a man would live (8:1) he must obey this word (6); "it is your life" (32:47).

This is also prophetic teaching: "I will bring famine on the country, a famine not of bread, a drought not of water, but of hearing the word of Yahweh" (Am 8:11). Having ignored the word of God in times of prosperity, the people will experience the lack of it in times of crisis. The day of trouble reveals how strong are the inner springs and resources.

Jesus, at the time of his temptation (Mt 4:4), used this background to express his confidence in his Father and his detachment from anything but his Father's will, his spiritual food. The word of God is more vital to man's existence than the food he eats. Our Lord defines symbolically all his activity under the symbol of eating and drinking, giving us by his example the foundation of our personal ethics.

To his Apostles who are surprised at his lack of interest in food, when the morning's journey surely had sharpened his appetite, Jesus answered: "My food is to do the will of the one who sent me and to complete his work" (Jn 4:34). This saying goes far beyond Mt 4:4; Jesus' food is continually to do his Father's will, thus bringing to perfection the work given him, the salvation of men. In these words Jesus sums up his entire career, his mission, his aim, and his purpose. This is one of the

most important ideas of John's Christology. His concept
of the unity of the Father and the Son is first and fore-
most in terms of moral unity. It is this complete obedience of Jesus to his Father, which justifies Jesus' unique
claim of men's allegiance. This theme of bread as a type
of the teaching from heaven is treated at length in John's
chapter 6 where from the material bread, the multiplied
loaves, our Lord passes to the bread of his teaching, and
ultimately to the bread which is his very body.

In fact, the New Testament presents the mission of
Jesus along Incarnational lines. "You who wanted no
sacrifice or oblation, prepared a body for me" (Heb 10:5)
was the prayer of Jesus "on coming into the world."
And he adds, "Lo, I have come to obey your will" (7).
And the author of the epistle concludes: "And by that
will we have been sanctified through the offering of the
body of Jesus Christ made once and for all" (10). The
offering of Jesus' body means the same as the shedding
of his blood: each expresses the total self-offering of
himself. The entire life of Jesus was a life of commitment
and dedication. The cross is the climax, the culminating
expression of a life wholly concentrated on the will of
God. At the last Supper all Christian worship and ethics
are given in capsule form: "Do this in memory of me."
By placing all his activity under the sign of eating Jesus
makes obedience something vital and even joyful. Love
is as vital and permanent as the need for food: lack of
love, disobedience is consequently malnutrition or famine. Jesus is a man, a worker for whom food is the origin
and purpose of labor, a need as well as a joy. In this light
the words of Jesus take on new meaning: "This is the
work of God that you believe in him whom he has sent"
(Jn 6:29). "Do not labor for the food which perishes, but
for the food which endures to eternal life, which the Son
of Man will give you" (27). Faith in the Eucharistic bread
sums up our practical Christian living.

The symbolism of drinking for Jesus is equally important. To drink a cup of wine for Jesus is first of all an image for one's lot in life, doing God's will. "Father, take this cup away from me, but let it be as you, not I, would have it" (Mk 14:36). It also has here, as in Mk 10:38, the suggestion of overwhelming, unspeakable suffering. To the sons of Zebedee Jesus said: "You do not know what you are asking. Can you drink the cup that I am going to drink?" (Mk 10:38). This is clearly a reference to Christ's coming suffering and death.

At the Last Supper, after having eaten the bread, and taken the cup of his Father's will, Jesus gives himself in Person as food and drink. The Father nourishes his Son who in turn provides for his Church the Christian food and drink, his own body and blood.

To eat the body of Christ is first to recognize our limitations, and our dependence on him. It gives a spiritual meaning to our dinner table which is already a natural symbol of our daily needs and of the hard task of providing for them. Each Communion should make us realize our need for God and our dependence on him. To eat the body of Christ is also less a self-service than participation in a family meal. As St. Paul puts it, we should always act in such a way that the result is the building up of the body of Christ (1 Cor 10:23). And, in any case, "the kingdom of God does not mean food and drink but righteousness, peace and joy in the Holy Spirit" (Rm 14:17). What matters in the Eucharist is love and its expression in righteousness, peace, joy, and mutual service.

The symbolism of drinking also has importance for us Christians. "Drink of it, all of you," Jesus said. The Eucharistic wine is first of all a recall of our redemption, the cup of Christ's blood shed that man's sins may be forgiven. As we drink the cup we should remember the age-old principle that "without the shedding of blood there is no forgiveness of sins" (Heb 9:22. Christ shed his blood; his disciples must expect to bleed once in a while, or as the gospels put it, "to take up his cross and follow" Jesus (Mt 16:24). The cross for the followers of Jesus means loyalty to him and to his principles.

To drink Christ's blood is also to receive the enthusiasm which the Holy Spirit brings. Paul advised the Romans to replace drunkenness by the fullness of the Spirit. "Do not get drunk with wine but be filled with the Spirit, addressing one another in psalms and hymns and spiritual songs, singing and making melody to the Lord in your heart" (Ep 5:18-19). The real stimulus for effective living does not come from wine but from allowing the Holy Spirit full possession of the heart, an experience connected with joy, courage, spirituality and character. The wine of the Eucharistic chalice will do all that for it is the spirit that gives it life (Jn 6:63), the life that our Lord promised we will find in his flesh and blood: "The bread that I shall give is my flesh for the life of the world" (Jn 6:51).

For Christ to drink the bitter cup of God's will was to pass from this world to his Father. "Jesus knew that the hour had come for him to pass from this world to the Father. He had always loved those who were his in the world, but now showed how perfect his love was" (Jn 13:1). According to a Jewish tradition the word Passover meant a passing or crossing over, referring it to the crossing of the Red Sea (Ex 14). By his death, Christ, and we with him, passed from this world, which is enslaved by sin, to the Father's company, the true promised land. By the Eucharist, a Christian's death loses its fearful character, and like Christ's, becomes a return to the Father. It is no longer a simple thing of the future but a spiritual event similar to the Lord's Passover. A believer's death is anticipated in his daily acts of renunciation. "If any man would come after me, let him deny himself and take up his cross daily and follow me" (Lk 9:23). In

the celebration of the Eucharist we find the glory of the
cross. "Death is swallowed up in victory. Death, where
is your victory? Death, where is your sting?" (1 Cor 15:
55). Death like a venomous serpent can no longer harm
those who are in Christ. Because we eat the body of
Christ we need no longer choose between life and death,
law and liberty, fear and love, our Lord and our Spouse,
son and servant, obedience and spontaneity, pain and joy,
sacrifice and feast, Jesus and the Spirit. Christ's supreme
love manifested in the Eucharist is the uniting force in
a Christian's life. "I am certain of this: neither death nor
life, no angel, no prince, nothing that exists, nothing still
to come, nor any power, or height or depth, nor any
created thing, can ever come between us and the love of
God made visible in Christ Jesus our Lord" (Rm 8:38-39).
The love of God is the unshakable foundation of Christian
life and hope. A loving Lord guards and guides us
through all the unknown contingencies of the present
and of the future.

"I am God's wheat and I am grinded by the teeth of
the beasts to become the pure bread of Christ." This
phrase of St. Ignatius of Antioch underlines the Eucharistic character of every Christian's life. It relates closely
the gesture of our holy Communion and the service and
love that we must constantly extend to our fellow man.
A Christian lets himself be eaten, he gives himself to his
neighbor as Christ gives himself to all of us. This exem-
plarism is a favorite Johannine idea. Just as the Father,
so also the Son; just as the Son, so also the disciple; just
as the Father and the Son, so also the Church. "As the
Father has loved me, so I have loved you" (Jn 15:8). "Just
as I have loved you, you also must love one another"
(13:34). "Father, may they be one in us, as you are in
me and I am in you" (17:21).

We find a similar idea in Jn 7:37 where there is a
promise of living water. "Jesus cried out: If any man is

thirsty let him come to me! Let the man come and drink who believes in me! As Scripture says: From his breast shall flow fountains of living water. He was speaking of the Spirit which those who believe in him were to receive" (Jn 7:37-39). The liturgy of the feast of Tabernacles which forms the background of these words, included prayers for rain, rites which commemorated the Mosaic water-miracle (Ex 17:1-7). For seven days water was carried in a golden pitcher from the Pool of Siloam to the temple as a reminder of the water from the rock in the desert (Nb 20:2-13) and as a symbol of hope for the coming Messianic deliverance. Jesus is the true water of life, who turns the symbol into reality. "From his breast" (Jn 7:38) is referred by many Fathers to "the man who believes in me" and not directly to Christ, making the streams flow from the believer who becomes a channel of life to others, through Christ's Spirit given at Pentecost. The supplies of water are in the believer (Jn 4:14), though they will of course be in him only because Christ is in him. The idea of flowing water irrigating the land is a vivid reminder of the way in which truth is communicated and is beneficial. The believer cannot end in satisfying his own thirst; he at once becomes a fount whence others may derive refreshment. Whether he wills to be a teacher or not, the true Christian cannot fail to impart the spirit of Christianity to others. And even if John did not have the disciple directly in mind but Christ, the implicit sense of the passage would still be the one suggested. The dilemma is textual not spiritual. Christ is the origin of the river of the Spirit. To believe in him is to slake our thirst for truth, hope, and love. The water that Christ gives becomes in the believer a spring welling up to eternal life (Jn 4:14). Jesus' gift is God's life in man. "Water living and speaking in me, and saying to me from within, Come to the Father," is how Ignatius of Antioch puts it. The Christian, however,

is never alone in the Church; we all "belong to Christ
and Christ belongs to God" (1 Cor 3:23). All are members
of Christ's body and mutually of one another. The Christian's life must reflect this community of interest and
duty of service.

Finally, the Christian must be ready to eat and drink
with any one, like Christ who stands at the door knock-
ing. "If one of you hears me calling and opens the door,
I will come in to share his meal, side by side with him"
(Rv 3:20). The Eucharist is the source of a universal love
which is at ease at all tables and is host to all who are
looking for bread, especially the bread of which earthly
bread is but a sample, a symbol. The bread of life, however, can be the occasion of condemnation if it is received
without recognizing the body of the Lord (1 Cor 11:29),
just like Judas' kiss at Gethsemane signified treason. The
Eucharist introduces us into a world of contrasts where
the commonplace becomes full of wonders and the marvelous can be the occasion of the greatest calamity. It is
salvation for believers but also a stumbling block for
those who refuse life. And in all this Eucharistic action
the Christian has a part: "Do this in memory of me."

12.

THE TWO TABLES

How does one encounter Christ nowadays? What signs make him recognizable? Some are saying, "I meet him in other people, in working for the community of man." For others he is in the center of all spiritual sharing, especially in the experience of shared prayer: "Christ is clearly there, one can feel it!" And what is curious, strange, inexplicable in these attitudes is that the presence of Christ in the Eucharist is seldom referred to; not that it is systematically doubted, yet it is practically ignored, apparently because its dynamic force is no longer felt. Yet the Eucharistic presence is the highest form of Christ's presence to his Church. It is not, however, a static presence separated from the other modes of presence.

There is only one presence of Christ according to his proper mode of existence and that is at God's right hand (Heb 10:12); all other presences are secondary. And just as there is just one subject of presence, the person of the Word Incarnate, there is really only one presence of Christ in different ways, which are all real presences and sacramental presences, although the qualifiers sacramental and real belong to the Eucharistic presence by antonomasia, par excellence, pre-eminently.

The presence of Christ is also of its very nature a personal presence, a communication from the person of Christ to the person of the Christian. We are not dealing with a mental abstraction but with a living person or at least with a living force or power emanating from a living person. There are as many real presences of Christ as there are grounds for this communication; and the presence is more real and perfect the more perfect is the basis or reason which makes him present to us. Moreover in the Eucharist, as in the Incarnation, bodily presence and personal presence cannot be separated.

The substantial presence of Christ in the Eucharist is the highest possible form of presence short of the beatific vision. It is the presence of the whole Christ, of his humanity and of his divinity. Every other presence of Christ is by way of effective causality. The agent is in the recipient of his action by means of the effect produced. Thus Christ is present by virtue of his efficacious, energizing power in the other sacraments, in the liturgical acts of worship, in his word, in the prayer of the Church gathered in his name, in the acts of beneficence performed out of love for him.

Every operative presence of Christ refers back and proceeds from the Incarnate Word who is in heaven according to his natural mode of being, but also sacramentally in the holy Eucharist, the Eucharist being a privileged center of operation here below. And every earthly presence of Christ is ordained to the increase of Christ's spiritual presence in us. In particular, the intended result of the Eucharist being the fervor of charity, our communion with Christ should be like a flash of fire, enkindling in us the presence of the one who knows and loves us (Rv 1:5) as we strive to know and love him better. "Christ passes through our mouth to reach our heart. It is better for you to have him in your mind than in your stomach" (Hugh of St. Victor). Hence the special excellence of the actual spiritual presence of Christ in our soul by which, in faith and love, Christ gives himself to us in the Holy Spirit.

The role of the indwelling Spirit is paramount in any

of the manifold presences of Christ. The Holy Spirit is the climate, the atmosphere, the pervading influence, the previous condition for the actual presence of Christ. It is only in the Holy Spirit that one can pray, hope, and love, that the mutual presence of Christ and of the faithful can be realized and intensified. And again, the presence of God's grace in our heart is the purpose of all Christ's presences in our life, and most especially of his Eucharistic presence.

There are then many ways of encountering Christ: in others, in world events, in everyday life; in the Church, the community, the people with whom we live and work; in my conscience, in my heart; in his Word, the Bible, the Gospel; in the sacraments and especially in the most Blessed Sacrament.

The world is a sacrament, a sign of God, but an image that is often deformed if not completely marred, disfigured. It does not suffice to be born to the world, to be reborn in God's grace, to be a sign of his kingdom. And while it is certain that Christ is present in every truly Christian encounter, it is not always clear that my relations with my neighbor are an authentic gesture of fraternal love. Every human act is limited and marked with the ambiguity of our present human condition. My brother is a sacrament of Christ, but human liberty easily obscures Christ's presence and may even reduce considerably its credibility.

Christ is present in the community provided the community is really a cell in the body of Christ and is really united in his name. The same is true for the prayer I formulate in my heart (Mt 6:6). I must pray in Christ's name (Jn 15:16), fraternally united to the prayer of his Church, and as a member of his body. My interior life cannot be allowed to degenerate into self-complacency.

The word of God to be living, energizing (Heb 4:12) must be received in faith (1 Th 1:6), it must grow (1 Jn

3:9) and be our nourishment (Rv 10:9). I will meet Christ
in his word, if I read it in his Spirit, and if I strive to
live by it.

The sacraments are all acts of Christ; yet even they
are always ambiguous signs since they depend largely
on the way every person participates in the coming of
the kingdom, on the quality of our communion to the
Spirit of our Lord. Just as "no one can say Jesus is Lord,
unless he is under the influence of the Holy Spirit" (1 Cor
12:3), so also without the same Spirit no one can say,
"Jesus is there." And there is possibility of indefinite
growth in the Spirit.

In the Eucharistic presence, objectively every ambiguity is lifted even if Christ is present in a veiled manner,
and through the sacramental signs, and in the domain of
faith and not of vision. The Eucharist is our viaticum, our
food for our earthly journey, a sign of hope for a pilgrim
people. But here also the valid sacrament is not auto-
matically fruitful. The members of the Eucharistic assembly must be converted to Jesus Christ "for the life of the
world" (Jn 6:51). This is how the Eucharist is the summit
and source (PO, no. 5) of everything that is Christian:
summit to which converge all the events of history, the
life of the Church, personal prayer, the preaching of the
word, and the administration of the sacraments; the
source at which all life is renewed.

The ambiguity of the signs of Christ's presence is not
due only to the quality of the believer's faith but also to
the discretion of the risen Lord who does not want to
impose himself but leaves men write their own history
"feeling their way towards him" (Ac 17:27). It is only in
the heavenly banquet of God's kingdom that we will
understand the value of all our repeated, provisional
Eucharists; it is only in the Eucharistic Christ that all
our gestures of solidarity, all our attempts at fraternal
union take on their real meaning.

Briefly, all the presences of Christ have their ambiguity because of the human recipient of Christ's gift of himself. Yet two presences stand out as exceptional because of their essentially objective nature, above all the Eucharistic presence but also Christ's presence in Scripture as the ultimate object, the Word of God's inspired revelation. And both of these presences are conveniently united in the Eucharistic celebration.

One of the most important elements in the recent liturgical renewal is unquestionably the publication of the new lectionaries, dominical and ferial. The Constitution on the Liturgy gives the theological thinking on which this new emphasis on the Word of divine revelation is grounded. "Christ is present in his word since it is he himself who speaks when the Holy Scriptures are read in Church" (SC, no. 7). "The two parts which make up the Mass, namely, the Liturgy of the Word and the Eucharistic Liturgy, are so closely connected with each other that they form one single act of worship" (no. 56).

"Sacred Scripture is of paramount importance in the celebration of the liturgy. For it is from Scripture that lessons are read and explained in the homily, and psalms are sung: the prayers, collects, and liturgical songs are scriptural in their inspiration, and it is from Scripture that actions and signs derive their meaning. Thus if the restoration, progress, and adaptation of the sacred liturgy are to be achieved, it is necessary to promote that warm and living love for Scripture to which the venerable tradition of both Eastern and Western rites gives testimony" (no. 24).

The priest is first of all a minister of the Word. "The people of God finds its unity first of all through the Word of the living God. No one can be saved who has not first believed. Priests have as their primary duty the proclamation of the gospel of God to all men. Thus they establish and build up the people of God. Through the saving Word the spark of faith is struck in the hearts of unbelievers; by this faith the community of the faithful is born and grows, as the Apostle says, 'Faith depends on hearing and hearing on the word of Christ'" (Rm 10:17; PO, no. 4).

The Church is then God's people assembled by the Word, to hear the Word, and in the Eucharist obey his word, his invitation at the Last Supper: "Do this in memory of me." All liturgy, all Christian prayer is the acceptance and the answer to this word in faith. The believer is first of all the one who has received God's word in a good and generous heart (Lk 8:15). To pray, to celebrate the Eucharist is to have the certitude that God has not ceased to speak to us, today as well as yesterday.

Christ is the Word made flesh, who by all his existence realized God's word in the biblical sense. He is the fulfillment and the truth of all the Scriptures; he is the term of a long history, a long tradition. And this fulfillment finds its climax in the tradition, the handing over, the surrender of his body and of his blood. Thus God's Word is embodied into an action, and this action finds all its meaning in the Word from which it derives. This is the fundamental structure of every sacrament and in accord with the best psychology. We are at the same word and action; our actions are ambiguous if they are not explicitated by our words; our words are equivocal if they are not confirmed by our deeds. With the body and blood of Christ we receive the totality of the Christian message, "all the spiritual treasure of the Church" (PO, no. 6).

The Eucharistic liturgy is the realization of the Word of God, it makes it real and operative. The gesture of Christ at the Last Supper is so full of meaning that it needs to be explained. The word **this** in the Lord's command, summarizes the whole of God's salvation history in Christ. Jesus was himself, according to the wonderful prologue of the Epistle to the Hebrews, the end result of all the experience of God's people.

The proclamation of the Word in the first part of the celebration, should help us to plumb the unfathomable riches hidden in the sacramental partaking of the body and blood of our Lord. As we enter into communication with the living Christ, he unveils little by little the beauty of his face and the traits of his personality. The overtones of the mystery of the new and eternal covenant are multiple. It is always with Christ dead and risen again that we have communion, we always share in his Passover. But during the Paschal season, Christ also reminds us, at Ascension time, that he already leads us with himself to the Father; and at Pentecost, that he draws us into the communion of the Holy Spirit. During Advent and the Christmas season, the Lord already transfigures our existence; he comes to live his Incarnation in us as he gives us his body and blood. During the ordinary liturgical time, he gives himself as our good Samaritan, as the one who invites his disciples to follow him, or as our healer. He repeats for us the wonders already announced under the Old Covenant, and which he worked for his contemporaries.

The word of God comes true in the Blessed Sacrament; the bread and the wine, fruit of the earth and work of human, prayerful hands, are consecrated by the power of the Spirit, who actualizes the events of the past. "That we might live no longer for ourselves but for him, he sent the Holy Spirit from you, Father, as his first gift to those who believe, to complete his work on earth and bring us the fullness of grace" (Eucharistic Prayer IV). Christ needs the realities of our daily life as the sacrament of his word; he is present in the Eucharist to make us the sacrament of his presence: "By your Holy Spirit gather all who share this bread and wine into the one body of Christ" (Eucharistic Prayer IV). As we hear the word of God in the Eucharistic liturgy we proclaim the demands of Christ's Incarnation and already are at work for their realization.

God's word is spoken through temporal realities to unveil the ultimate meaning of our existence. He becomes part of all that makes our life and of all our human history. That is the message of the Bible taken as a whole; it includes all human feelings, all our trials and all our joys. The liturgy places them all in the context of the totality of the Christian mystery which is concentrated in the gift of the body of Christ, during the course of the liturgical year with its various readings.

Nothing can worthily replace the word of God in the Eucharistic celebration. The celebration of the Eucharist is not primarily the celebration, the sacralization of our human life, but the celebration of the mystery of Christ's death and resurrection, and the celebration of the action of God in our life, an action which constantly impels us to further progress.

To hear God's word and to receive Christ's body is to enter little by little into the life of the Spirit. It is to reduce the distance that separates us from the day when Christ will be all in all. The Eucharist effectively looks forward to and hopes for the one kingdom where the word of God will be fully realized in each one of us. This eschatological dimension of the Eucharist is emphasized in the Constitution on the Sacred Liturgy. "It is through the liturgy, especially the divine Eucharistic sacrifice, that the work of our redemption is exercised. The liturgy is thus the outstanding means by which the faithful can express in their lives, and manifest to others the mystery of Christ and the real nature of the Church . . . Day by day the liturgy builds up those within the Church into the Lord's holy temple, into a spiritual dwelling for God (Ep 2:21-22), an enterprise which will continue until Christ's full stature is achieved (Ep 4:13). At the same time the liturgy marvelously fortifies the faithful in their capacity to preach Christ" (SC, no. 2). The Eucharist is the efficacious sign of and a distant preparation for Christ's future parousia; in it we proclaim Christ's Paschal mystery until he comes again in glory (1 Cor 11:26).

Christ, especially in the Eucharist, is the sacrament of our encounter with God, a visible sign effective of our salvation through our faith. The Church also is a sacrament by being like Christ a servant among men, the servant of men in view of Christ. As servant of the grace of Christ's kingdom, the Church coordinates and realizes all the signs of Christ's presence to his people. The people of God in turn become the sacrament both of the Church and of Christ by assimilating in faith and love the fruits of Christ's presence to his Church in the Holy Spirit to the Father's glory.

13.

CHRIST'S SACRIFICE AND OURS

Scarcely any religion is known that does not have a sacrificial ritual. In general, sacrifice can be described as a material oblation made with the purpose of establishing or maintaining communion with the deity. The ceremonial act is an acknowledgment that everything belongs to God, and at the same time an expression of the desire to draw near to God. Each religion supplies its own specific explanation of the act of sacrifice. In Israel, the holocaust and the communion sacrifice were the two most ancient sacrificial rites, and clearly show what Israel intended by its sacrifices.

In the holocaust, as described in Lv (ch. 1), the victim was completely burnt. The imposition of the offerer's hands on the victim's head (1:4) was a solemn attestation that the offerer identified himself with the victim which later was presented to the priest. In Lv 1:5 the holocaust is given an expiatory value; in ancient times it was rather a sacrifice of thanksgiving (1 S 6:14, 10:8) or a sacrifice to obtain a divine favor (1 S 7:9). The holocaust was an act principally of homage expressed through total sacrifice to God, an act of devotion and submission, a recognition of God's universal sovereignty. The offering being wholly consumed on the altar signified the complete self-surrender of the offerer to God. God's acceptance of the sacrifice is expressed anthropomorphically by the sweet, agreeable odor (Lv 1:13) rising from the burnt victim.

The communion sacrifice (Lv, ch. 3) was a covenant

meal in which the worshipper was sacramentally related
to God and to fellow Israelites. Joy and union with God
and with his faithful characterized the rite (Ne 8:10).
In both the holocaust and the communion sacrifice the
main idea was not one of destruction or of privation, but
of communion between God and man, a notion of God's
presence and influence in man's life, with the added idea
in the communion sacrifice that communion with our
brothers goes with communion with God. To put it briefly, in the Old Testament the ends of sacrifice in relation
to God were adoration, thanksgiving, expiation, and
petition.

Expiation for sin stands out in a special way in the
great day of Atonement (Yom Kippur), the yearly ritual
of atonement with the scapegoat ceremony (Lv 16). The
yearning for expiation expressed in such ancient rituals
is fully satisfied by the unique sacrifice of Christ (Heb
9:6-14). Paul says that through the free gift of God's grace
we have been redeemed "in Christ Jesus whom God
destined to be a propitiatory through faith by his blood"
(Rm 3:25). In the Old Testament the propitiatory is also
called the throne of mercy (Ex 25:17). It is presented as
a golden cover for the Ark of the Covenant. Yahweh
appears on the propitiatory as on a throne (1 S 4:4) and
there speaks to Moses (Ex 25:22). On the day of Atonement the propitiatory was incensed and sprinkled with
blood (Lv 16:13, 15). In 1 Ch 28:11 the holy of holies is
called "the room for the throne of mercy."

The blood of Christ has performed what the ancient
ritual could only symbolize. His is the blood of the new
covenant (Ex 24:8) on Calvary but also in the Eucharist
(Mt 26:28). Christ's cross is the new mercy seat and on
the first Good Friday, the pre-eminently Christian day
of atonement, Christ, sprinkled with his own blood, is
the real propitiatory, the Father's means of wiping out
man's sins. The Old Testament propitiatory was but a

type of the Crucified Christ (Heb 9:5). God is always the same, always loving and compassionate towards his creatures; but sin interposes a barrier which prevents man from receiving the full benefits of God's love, a barrier which the perfect self-dedication of Christ, expressed through the shedding of his blood, has now swept away.

All the life of Christ was a sacrifice since sacrifice is an offering, an act of worship made in view of communion with God. Christ coming into the world recognized that his obedience is the only sacrifice agreeable to God (Heb 10:5-6), and so in full submission he offered himself to his Father: "God, here I am, I am coming to obey your will" (7). By this gracious act he voluntarily identified himself with humanity to such an extent that his life of total obedience to the Father, even to the point of dying on the cross (Ph 2:8), becomes the ultimate act of obedience for all who acknowledge their identification with him. Christ's sacrifice was a sacrifice of obedience, the voluntary and glad surrender of his own life to God, in perfect communion with God's will. His daily bread is to do the will of the Father who sent him (Jn 4:34); and it was with a final act of obedience that he drank the bitter cup of his agony and death: "If this cup cannot pass away without my drinking it, your will be done" (Mt 26:42).

Christ adds something new to the Old Testament idea of sacrifice, namely, the identity between the priest and the victim. He is the one who offers and is offered to the Father. Christ introduces into the idea of sacrifice the primacy of the human over the ritualistic aspect. It is now less a question of performing acts of worship than of offering one's self, of a profound, interior transformation of all that we are, for the love of God.

This interiorization of sacrifice was already preached by the prophets and the psalmists, who emphasized the interior dispositions that must be behind acceptable sacrifice: obedience, gratitude, contrition. "What I want is love not sacrifice; knowledge of the law not holocausts" (Ho 6:6). "My sacrifice is this broken spirit, you will not scorn this crushed and broken heart" (Ps 51:17). A broken spirit is one in which the self-assertive craving for autonomy has been shattered and replaced by conformity to God's will. Jeremiah gives interiorization of religion as the characteristic of the new covenant: "I will make a new covenant. Deep within them I will plant my law, writing it on their hearts" (Jr 31:33). Our Lord alludes to this text at the Last Supper when he speaks of "the new covenant in his blood" (1 Cor 11:25). Ezechiel gave the precision that the new covenant would be a gift of the Spirit. "I shall give you a new heart and put a new spirit in you. I shall put my spirit in you and make you keep my laws" (Ezk 36:26-27). The Holy Spirit will be the principle inspiring the new covenant. This effusion of the spirit will be effected through Christ who will be the first recipient of it, to be able to accomplish his saving work. He alone lives of the plentitude of the Spirit; he alone is in the strict sense, the Son begotten to the Father by the Holy Spirit. "He offered himself as the perfect sacrifice to God through the eternal Spirit" (Heb 9:14). The eternal Spirit here is the divine power and sanctity taking hold of Christ's human nature. As the Savior depended upon the power and direction of the Holy Spirit to accomplish the will of the Father in all his life, so he did in death. United with Christ in his self-offering, the Christian shares in true worship, which is dedication of himself to God's service in union with Jesus Christ, the offering of himself as a spiritual sacrifice after the model of Christ.

All the life of Christ was a sacrifice but his death was the climax of his self-dedication to God to whom he commends his dying spirit (Lk 23:46); his death was also the final demonstration of his love for us men. "A man

can have no greater love than to lay down his life for
his friends" (Jn 15:13). Christ thought of his approaching
death as a sacrifice on behalf of others. His death puts
the seal of authenticity on his sacrificial life. It was not
an accident but in full continuity with the rest of his life.
Fidelity to his mission brought Christ to his death. And
his death is intimately related to his resurrection, which
is the positive element of his sacrifice, the final and full
communion with God, God's acceptance of Christ's sacrifice and the climactic achievement in the saving deeds of
Christ. Not until he has received the fullness of the life
which is properly his as Son of God and son of man, not
until in his own person are exhibited the full fruits of
the new life he confers by his redeeming act, is the
redemptive work complete and effective. "Jesus Christ
our Lord was proclaimed Son of God in power through
his resurrection from the dead" (Rm 1:4). Paul attributes
Christ's resurrection to God's power, which establishes
him as Kyrios, Lord, deserving anew, this time in virtue
of his Messianic work, the name he had from all eternity,
Son of God. By the resurrection God officially installed
him as Messianic King. The resurrection is the heavenly
enthronement of the Messiah King.

For us Christians, as for Christ himself, all our Christian life is a sacrifice. For us as for Christ, there is identity between the priest and the victim. It is ourselves
that we must offer, with Christ and in Christ, of course,
but our very life must be the subject matter of our worship in spirit and in truth. "Come to him, to that stone
rejected by men but in God's sight chosen and precious;
and like living stones be yourselves built into a spiritual
house, to be a holy priesthood, to offer spiritual sacrifices
acceptable to God through Jesus Christ" (1 P 2:4-5).
Christ is the rock of destiny: to those who believe he is
chosen and precious in God's sight because of the new
life he shares with those who come to him; to those who

reject him he is a rock that makes them fall, a stumbling
block (1 P 2:8). The images are mixed: a spiritual house
is being built of living stones, then a holy priesthood is
offering spiritual sacrifices. The ancient holy people was
formed around Mt. Sinai but could not approach it. The
new people of God gather around another rock which
can be approached, Christ who is the basis and standard
on which God erects his building stone by stone. So also
the spiritual sacrifices of the Christians replace the sacrifices which had sealed the ancient covenant. Finally, the
image of growth replaces that of structure. Jesus had
compared himself to the stone rejected by the Jewish
builders, but chosen by God (Mt 21:42). The Christians
are living stones like him, being built into a spiritual
edifice, the Church, where they render to God in Christ,
the only worship worthy of him. They form a new temple
in which the bonding material, the bond of union, is not
race but the Spirit. To come to Christ involves incorporation into that community which belongs to him, shares
his election, and is the living temple of which he is the
living foundation stone. This community is the new Israel
(1 P 2:9) whose two-fold function is to offer to God
through Christ the spiritual sacrifice of its obedience
(1 P 2:5), of a life based on Christian faith, and to show
forth God's mighty works (1 P 2:9). Christ is the living
stone not merely because he is a person but because as
risen Lord, he is endowed with new life and is life-
giving, our source of life. Christians are to grow continually in their union with him. The essential part of any
sacrifice, even in the Old Testament, lay in its spiritual
nature, the disposition of the offerers. Such was the value
of the sacrifice of Christ, and the Christian sacrifices can
only be acceptable to God so far as they are united to
Christ's and bear the same character.

Note that all the terms are corporate: to be a Christian is to live within the community of God's people.

By constant communion with Christ, the living stone, Christians will become like him living stones. The purpose of stones is not to be kept in isolation but so to be joined together as to form a building. This, however, describes only one aspect of the corporate life and by itself is insufficient as a description, for once built into an edifice, the stone's role is passive. So Peter switches thought from the structure, presumably the temple, to those who actively function inside the building in corporate worship: here is the active side of the life of the Christian family. The sacrificial system is spiritualized by the offering of the whole life and self of the Christian in union with Christ to the service of God.

"I appeal to you therefore, brethren, by the mercies of God, to present your bodies as a living sacrifice, holy and acceptable to God, which is your spiritual worship" (Rm 12:1). The Christian community replaces the Temple of Jerusalem, and the Holy Spirit who dwells therein gives a new intensity to God's presence in the midst of his holy people. He inspires a new spiritual worship, since believers are members of Christ who in his crucified and risen body, has become the place of a new presence of God and of a new worship (Jn 2:21). God's redeeming love should be answered by the true sacrifice and spiritual ritual service of a life of purity and self-denial and work for God. Christian living has all the associations of the resurrected life which is living indeed. Worship in this sense is the whole life. It is our adoring response to God, of whose mercies we are aware. Everything a Christian does can be worship.

In this background it remains to be seen what the Eucharist meant for Jesus and what it should mean for us. The presentation of all Christ's life as sacrificial does not exclude in any way the special offering of his body and blood, which gave full expression to his will; nor does it exclude any holy action by which Christians iden-

tify themselves with his action, especially in the celebration of the Eucharist. The statement of true worship as
embracing the whole of the Christian's life from day to
day does not exclude the importance of the congrega-
tional assembly which is worship's focal point. No biblical statement on the necessity of interiorizing worship
ever was meant or understood as excluding the external
manifestations of worship.

For Christ the Eucharist was a clear statement of
purpose, the explanation to his disciples and to all men,
of the meaning of his death. This is Christ's body given,
sacrificed for all men, the blood shed for our redemption
(Lk 22:19-20). If Jesus had not celebrated the Last Supper, he would have left us a sealed mystery. The Eucharist is our legacy, Christ's bequest in our favor. "Take
and eat, this is my body given for you." He is to the end
the Servant of his brothers. Giving himself he unites us
to him, he includes us in his sacrifice and gives us the
means of assimilating its fruits, of "proclaiming his death
until he comes again" (1 Cor 11:26). The Last Supper
shows Jesus on the royal road to the cross, in full liberty
and without any coercion. "I lay down my life in order to
take it up again. No one takes it from me, I lay it down
of my own free will" (Jn 10:18). The Eucharist is not
only the announcement of Christ's death but also of his
resurrection: "the bread that I shall give is my flesh for
the life of the world" (Jn 6:51).

For us the Mass is not the ritual expression of our
sacrifices but Christ's sacrifice that we try to live in our
own small way. Our life must be a life of faith and of
spiritual worship, but the Mass is the mystery of faith,
its highest summit. Our life must be a sharing of ourselves with our brothers, and that also is part of our
spiritual worship. Now this sharing takes place first of
all in the Eucharist which builds up the mystical body of
Christ, since the essential purpose of the sacrament is

the fervor of Christian love. The first of our spiritual
sacrifices is to accept living as members of Christ's body;
and when we come together to do so, we not only show
what we are, but also the source and origin of our life.
"That we might live no longer for ourselves but for him,
he sent the Holy Spirit from you, Father, as his first gift
to those who believe, to complete his work on earth and
bring us the fullness of grace . . . By your Holy Spirit
gather all who share this bread and wine into the one
body of Christ, a living sacrifice of praise" (Eucharistic
Prayer IV).

14.

COMMUNION I

The principal effect of the reception of the Eucharist is a life of union with God through Christ, our Lord. "He who eats my flesh and drinks my blood, lives in me and I live in him. As I, who am sent by the living Father, myself draw life from the Father, so also whoever eats me will draw life from me" (Jn 6:56-57). The life that the Father communicates to the Son passes to the faithful through the Eucharist. The union of the faithful with Christ is realized in the highest degree in the Eucharist (1 Cor 10:16). The reception of the Eucharist is also the expression and the cause, the nourishment of Christian fellowship, the vital union of the faithful among themselves that arises from their union with Christ.

The term fellowship (in Greek **koinonia,** communion) keeps in its many different uses a fundamental meaning. The basic idea in fellowship is that of possessing something in common, that is, the notion of participation, partnership, or sharing. Christian fellowship, or communion, means sharing a common life in Christ through the Holy Spirit. It binds believers to one another, but the important thing is that it binds them also and especially to God, by sharing the divine life, the communion of the Father and of the Son in the Holy Spirit.

Communion has its source in the realities that are possessed in common by different persons, material or spiritual realities. Actually among Christians material goods are always joined with spiritual benefits. Paul, for

example, says that the pagans, who share the spiritual
blessings of the Jews, have the duty to help them with
temporal possessions (Rm 15:27). That is his constant
theme for the collection he organized in favor of the poor
Christian Jews in Jerusalem (2 Cor 9:13). The sharing
can consist in taking part in some action or in sharing
some sentiments. "We know that sharing our sufferings
you will also share our consolations" (2 Cor 1:7). Paul
insists constantly on the presence of antagonistic or even
contradictory realities in Christ, in the apostle, and in
the Christian: suffering and consolation, death and life,
poverty and riches, weakness and strength. This is the
Paschal mystery, the presence of the risen Christ in the
midst of the old world of sin and death. A Christian can
have no part of sin: "What fellowship has light with
darkness?" (2 Cor 6:14). Nor can he "become an accom-
plice in anybody else's sin" (1 Tm 5:22). He shares with
other Christians "in Jesus, the tribulation, the kingdom,
and the patient endurance" (Rv 1:9). The Christian's
whole life whether he suffers, reigns, or waits is in union
with Jesus. The placing of the kingdom between tribulation and patient endurance is eloquent of the firmness of
Christian hope, and also of the general New Testament
insistence that "through many tribulations we must
enter the kingdom of God" (Ac 14:22). Those who share
their Priest-King's sufferings will also share his sovereignty.

The word fellowship became characteristic, descrip-
tive of the first Christian community: "They remained
faithful to fellowship" (Ac 2:42, 4:32-37). Everywhere
there was a great sense of togetherness, a common life
under the leadership of the Apostles. What constitutes
this brotherhood or fellowship is a united purpose and
a care for the poorer members to the extent of holding
all goods in common, an openhearted sharing in which
each believer gave to others what he had himself re-

ceived, whether of spiritual or material blessings. Their community of goods was evidence of their unity of heart; their sharing was the expression of their unity and harmony as believers, manifesting their possession of the Spirit. Christian fellowship is not only mutual, social aid, common ideology, or just a sentiment of solidarity. It is the end result of the sharing of the gospel and of all the benefits received from God through Jesus Christ in the apostolic community, especially the breaking of the bread. In one word, it is Christian charity, love of God and love of neighbor.

Fellowship with Christ, the Christian's life in Christ, is the communion from which all the others derive. "God is faithful, by whom you were called into the fellowship of his Son, Jesus Christ our Lord" (1 Cor 1:9). God's character guarantees the outcome of his call. God has called us to an ultimate and vital union with his Son through the gift of faith.

This communion with Christ gives us a share in goods that are strictly divine. St. Paul says that his apostolic work gives him a share in the blessings of the gospel (1 Cor 9:23). He tells the Philippians that he is grateful for their "partnership in the gospel" (Ph 1:5). They cooperated to spread the gospel not only by sending money but also by suffering for the good news, an important contribution to the apostolic witness (Ph 1:5). So also Philemon is told that his mercy to Onesimus, his runaway slave, would show to the world his sense of communion with Christ and with his brothers, a faith penetrated by charity. "I pray that the sharing of your faith may promote the knowledge of all the good that is ours in Christ" (Phm 6).

But sharing in God's own divine life is what is most important in our communion with Christ. Because Christ shared in our human nature (Heb 2:14) we are able to share in God's own nature. As a result of "the glory and

excellence of Christ," the miracles done by Jesus as a
sign of his divinity (Jn 1:14), in particular his transfiguration, and his excellence, that is, his natural and supernatural power, "you will be able to share the divine
nature" (2 P 1:4). This is one of the great texts of the
New Testament. "He was made man that we might be
made god" (Athanasius). It is the power of Christ that
lies behind the whole Christian life. Through his glory
and excellence Christ has founded our Christian hope.
The Christian, now by faith, later in the fulfillment of
the Parousia, is a partaker of the divine nature. Even
now the Christian can enjoy intimate union with Christ
and with the Father and with the Holy Spirit. He enjoys
intimate fellowship with them while awaiting its consummation on the last day.

The Christian life in Christ unites us "with the
Father and his Son Jesus Christ" (1 Jn 1:3). This will
mean sharing in Christ's sufferings. "All I want is to
know Christ and the power of his resurrection, and to
share his sufferings by reproducing the pattern of his
death" (Ph 3:10). The new life of the believer springs
from Christ's opened grave. To know Christ as risen and
living is to have power to suffer like him and for him,
and to possess the sure hope of rising and living with
him. All apostolic Christians living in the body of Christ
must share in his sufferings and thus contribute to the
growth of that body. This death to the world, assisted by
the Spirit, is a continuation of our baptism when we were
brought to a state of union with the suffering and dying
Christ (Rm 6:3-4). The power of the risen Christ is the
vital principle of the new Christian life, the new creation.
It gradually brings the man of faith into an image of
Christ himself and enables him to be identified with Jesus
in his sufferings, death, and resurrection. Being a partner
with Christ's sufferings means having one's existence
shaped by Christ's death in order to reach the resurrec-

tion life. To know Christ involves fellowship, obedience, and service. To have fellowship with Christ is to have the power of his resurrection in daily experience. To share in Christ's sufferings is to be associated with our Lord in his death in two ways. There is that identification with Christ in his death and resurrection that baptism signifies, a death to sin, and a new life with him and in him to righteousness. Leading on from that into the whole of Christian life and service, there is a sharing of his sufferings and death of which Jesus himself spoke (Mk 8:34-35) and in the willingness to suffer that his saving gospel may go out to all men. Those who share in Christ's sufferings are assured of having part also in his glory. "Rejoice in so far as you share Christ's sufferings, that you may also rejoice and be glad when his glory is revealed" (1 P 4:13).

The Holy Spirit also plays an important role in Christian spiritual living. This involves not only "the grace of the Lord Jesus Christ and the love of God" but also "the fellowship of the Holy Spirit" (2 Cor 13:13). This is the fullest of all Paul's references to the Triune God and its scope is unlimited. The order is significant. The grace of Christ leads one toward the love of God, and the love of God when actualized through the Spirit produces fellowship with God and man. The fellowship, the communication of the Holy Spirit is what he effects, the sense of his presence and guidance, the sense of unity within the Church which he bestows, the mutual love which he creates within the Christian community. First the grace of Christ, or the grace of God revealed through Christ, for thereby God's love has been apprehended, and therefrom the fellowship of the Holy Spirit has become a continuing reality. There can be no adequate understanding of God's love apart from the cross. Grace, chronologically first in Christian experience, brings the believer to know the love shown by God in Christ, and

thence to share in the fellowship of Christians brought
about and maintained by and in the Holy Spirit.

For St. Paul communion with God in Christ and in
the Holy Spirit results in our **adoption** as children of God.
Paul is the only New Testament writer who uses this
metaphor taken from Roman law. "Everyone moved by
the Spirit is a son of God. The Spirit you have received
is the spirit of sons and it makes us cry, Abba, Father!
We too groan inwardly as we await for adoption as sons,
the redemption of our bodies" (Rm 8:14, 23). Spirit-led
and God-adopted are qualifiers for the same group of
people whose lives are spent in the service not of an
owner whom they fear but of a father whom they love.
Adoption was not a widely practiced institution among
the Jews. Perhaps Paul borrowed the word from current
Hellenistic language to show how the baptized Christian
has been taken into God's family and has a status in it,
not of a slave, who indeed belonged to the household, but
of a son. Through the Spirit the Christian is able to proclaim in all truth that God is his Father.

The gift of the Spirit constitutes our adoption, and in
adopting us God gives us a participation in the sonship
of Christ. The Christian can then speak of God in the
very terms used by Christ, "Abba, Father." Uttered under the influence of the Spirit, the prayer of the believer
is a proof that God loves him as he loves his own Son,
and that the Father is the center and the end of the
Christian's prayer and of his life.

The spirit of sonship (literally adoption) is the spirit
of the Son transferred to the Christian; it enables him
to look at God with Christ's eyes and makes in him the
Son's own filial response to the Father, "Abba." It is the
Spirit who unites men to Christ and puts them in a
special relationship to the Father. The Spirit is not one
who maintains the frightening servile conditions of the
old era, but gives confidence that God is a personal

Father. And what has begun has yet to be completed when our bodies are set free at the resurrection and our full sonship is achieved. It is only the pledge of the full glory to come (Rm 8:23).

In referring to sonship Paul is not alluding only to the Hellenistic custom of adoption, but no doubt has Old Testament parallels in mind. Son or sons was a title for the Old Testament people of God: "They were adopted as sons" (Rm 9:4). Israel was Yahweh's covenant partner and chosen people. "Israel is my first-born Son" (Ex 4:22). Israel is the Lord's first-born son among the nations, a pre-eminent rank based upon divine adoption or election. Yahweh's love for Israel is that of a Father for his first-born son. The term first-born indicates the high honor conferred upon Israel and at the same time contains a hint of the ultimate inclusion of the Gentiles also in the covenant. This is the expression of one of the central Yahwistic themes, the election of Israel. "You are a people consecrated to Yahweh your God; it is you that Yahweh our God has chosen to be his very own people out of all the peoples of the earth" (Dt 7:6). Israel's election is not based on its greatness or goodness. The reason of God's choice is loyalty to the promises which, of his own loving will, he had made to the Fathers. Israel owes its status to God's grace alone. This choice ratified by the covenant makes Israel a dedicated people. Israel is a nation set apart, God's people, consecrated (Ex 19:6), a covenanted race, God's son (Dt 1:31), the nation of Emmanuel (Is 8:8). The notion of first-born first served to define the covenantal relationship (Dt 32:6). Hosea used fatherly love as a symbol for God's favors for Israel during the exilic period (Ho 11:1). The title first-born passed on to Christ who summed up in himself the destiny of Israel (Mt 2:15), and thus it passed to the Church through him and in him.

"God sent his Son to redeem the subjects of the law

and to enable us to be adopted as sons" (Gal 4:5). There are two aspects to redemption, a negative and a positive: the slave attains freedom by becoming a son. The adoption to sonship is not simply a legal right to inherit (7) but the real and inward giving of the divine life in which the three divine Persons are involved (2 Cor 13:13). "The proof that you are sons is that God has sent the Spirit of his Son into our hearts, the Spirit that cries, Abba, Father. And it is this that makes you a son, you are not a slave anymore" (Gal 4:6). Two analogies, redemption and adoption, describe the process by which men are put right with God. The status of sonship which Christ had by right of being the unique Son of God is granted to us by virtue of what he has done. The Father makes us sons by incorporating us in the Son.

Adoption is connected with the gift of the Spirit by which one is enabled to place his full confidence in and pledge his total commitment to God the Father. The gift of the Spirit is the constitutive element, the dynamic principle of Christian sonship. We acquire the status of sonship by sheer grace and gift. Sonship is vouchsafed to us through the indwelling Spirit who makes Christ a reality in our lives (Jn 15:26). The presence of the Holy Spirit in our hearts represents an entirely new attitude toward God. We come to him as children to a father.

God chose us and destined us to be his adopted sons in accord to his eternal purpose in Christ (Ep 1:5). Jesus Christ, the only Son, is both the source and the model of the way God has chosen us to become holy, that is, by adopting us as his heirs. Salvation comes to us by sharing Christ's unique sonship. The destination fixed for the believer is sonship, a purpose of divine love. In one sense, by creation, God is Father of all men, but the true sonship to him is a specifically Christian privilege bestowed by the Holy Spirit in the Church. It emphasizes both God's initiative in establishing a relationship with men and the character of that relationship: God's paternal love and man's responsibility to obey. God's love has as its purpose that there should be many sons in his family, all sharing the likeness of their brother (Rm 8:29). And the best way of being like Christ is to appropriate, assimilate his body and blood in the Eucharist and so to abide in him as he abides in us (Jn 6:56).

15.

COMMUNION II

Union with God and with our fellow men is the idea most central to John's teaching on Christian living. The central theme of our Lord's preaching was the kingdom of God, God's reign or sovereignty over his people, the theocratic ideal of the Old Testament. The Synoptics present the same teaching from a juridical viewpoint, stressing the identity of the two great commandments in the law, the love of God and the love of our neighbor (Mt 22:34-40). John, the mystic, looks at the end result, union with God and with our neighbor, and explains the inwardness of the spiritual life as a divine-human fellowship or communion. "What we have seen and heard we proclaim also to you, so that you may have fellowship with us; and our fellowship is with the Father and with his Son Jesus Christ" (1 Jn 1:3). John wishes to unite his readers with the Apostolic Church not simply in an orthodox confession, but rather in common love for God revealed in Christ. Union with the Church brings union with God. The unity of the Christian community is based on the union of each Christian with God in Christ; it is fellowship, oneness with Christ, as a branch in the vine. True life is communion with the Father and the Son, sharing in the fullness of eternal life that is in the Father and the Son; and it demands of men knowledge, pardon of sins, and moral obedience.

St. John describes our Christian life of union with God in different ways. By it a Christian **lives in God and**

God lives in him. "We can be sure that we are in God only when claiming to be living in him we live the same kind of life as Christ lived" (1 Jn 1:6). In this life we come closer to God through love than through knowledge, yet the apostolic catechesis concerning the mystery of Christ must be carefully received and prized. "If what you have heard from the beginning abides in you, then you will abide in the Son and in the Father" (1:24). If we keep God's word, both God's love for us and our love for him comes to perfection (1:5). "Whoever keeps his commandments lives in God and God lives in him" (3:24). "If we love one another God lives in us" (4:12).

"No one who abides in him sins" (1 Jn 3:6), because God living in the Christian is present with all his power for life. When a Christian sins he ceases to have that intimacy with God which alone gives meaning and reality to his Christian profession. Sin and the Christian are radically opposed and he must never be complacent about it, even about occasional sin. The life a man lives reveals the source from which he draws life. Sin for a Christian is an act completely out of character.

A further guarantee of the divine presence in us is the possession of the Holy Spirit. "We know that he lives in us by the Spirit that he has given to us" (1 Jn 3:24). The spirit is given, not earned, and he gives assurance. It is owing to the enlightenment given by the Holy Spirit that we abide in God. "We can know that we are living in him and he is living in us because he lets us share his Spirit" (1 Jn 4:13). It is God himself who through his Spirit produces charity in us.

Without the reality of the Christ-event as the exemplification of the divine love, Christian love is meaningless. "We have seen and testify that the Father has sent his Son as Savior of the world. If anyone acknowledges that Jesus is God, God lives in him and he in God" (4:14-15). As bases for communion with God faith and love are

inseparable. "God is love and anyone who lives in love
lives in God and God lives in him" (16). The mutual indwelling of vine and branches is in view (Jn 15:5); only
in the gospel it is the relation to Christ which is in view,
while here it is the relation to God in Christ. Finally the
life that the Father communicates to the Son passes to
the faithful through the Eucharist. "He who eats my
flesh and drinks my blood lives in me and I live in him.
As I who am sent by the living Father myself draw life
from the Father, so whoever eats me will draw life from
me" (Jn 6:56-57).

A Christian **begotten by God** has new life from him.
"You know that God is righteous; then you may be sure
that everyone who does right is born of him" (1 Jn 2:29).
Like father like son. The children of God will be recognized by righteous conduct, the standard of conduct being
God himself. The presence of righteous conduct is the
sure sign of the reality of the divine birth. Believers are
not simply worldly men who are trying to live a little
better. They are men who have been radically renewed.
They have been born all over again. The habitual practice of righteousness is evidence of such divine activity.

"No one born of God commits sin for God's seed remains inside him; he cannot sin because he is born of
God" (1 Jn 3:9). The seed of divine life introduced into
us by God is faith in the apostolic catechesis concerning
the mystery of Christ and fructified by the Holy Spirit
(2:20, 27). It is the new principle of life implanted at our
spiritual rebirth.

"Everyone who loves is born of God and knows God"
(1 Jn 4:7). Love, the eyes of the heart, is the organ of
perception of God. To love is characteristic of God's children as it is characteristic of God himself. "Whoever
believes that Jesus is the Christ has been begotten of
God" (5:1). The confession that Jesus is the Christ is not
the result of human insight. If a man makes it, it shows

that a divine work has taken place in him (1 Cor 12:3). The love that constitutes us children of God cannot exist apart from true Christian faith. Faith and love are inextricably interwoven. The one has no true existence without the other. Belief that Jesus is the Christ is not merely the acceptance of a dogma; it is a creative action by which men are so radically transformed that they exercise a victorious mastery over sin and the world. "We know that anyone who has been begotten by God does not sin because the begotten Son of God protects him, and the evil one does not touch him" (1 Jn 5:18). Christian belief and Christian life are inseparably linked. As a man believes, so he lives. As a man lives, so is his real belief.

The Christian is **from God;** he is God's child. "All that is in the world, the lust of the flesh and the lust of the eyes and the pride of life is not from the Father" (1 Jn 2:16). These are the motives that rule the world: unlawful physical gratification, sinful delights of mind or emotions, empty trust in possessions. The true realities are altogether different (2 Cor 4:18). All men are God's children by creation; as regards this a creature has no choice. But a creature endowed with free will can choose his own parent in the moral world. The Father offers him the power to become a child of God (Jn 1:12) but he can refuse this and become a child of the devil instead. There is no third alternative. Correspondence between spiritual parentage and moral character means that attitudes and actions manifest our spiritual nature.

"By this it may be seen who are the children of God, and who are the children of the devil: whoever does not do right is not from God, nor he who does not love his brother" (1 Jn 3:10). It is not enough to live a decent law-abiding life; there must also be that most excellent gift of charity, the special characteristic of Christ's followers.

St. John closes his epistle with a magisterial renun-

ciation of false doctrine, and at the same time a statement concerning the origin of believers: "We know that
we are from God" (1 Jn 5:19). He had previously stated:
"Children, you have already overcome these false prophets because you are from God and have in you one who
is greater than anyone in this world" (1 Jn 4:4).

In 1 Jn 4:4 **to know God** comes continually as a climax,
a highlight in our communion with God. To know God in
the Bible is to recognize and experience his power and
effective presence. It requires corresponding service and
love in man by keeping God's commandments and walking in his ways. This spiritual knowledge is manifested by
signs, by keeping the commandments, by holiness, belief,
and brotherly love. We know God through being born of
God, or being of God by the divine, dynamic seed of life
set in us to make us act like God. It goes with that abiding
in God and God in us, that presence of the Spirit which is
a share in the divine life and the principle of manifesta-
tory action, above all of love. Thus the Old Testament
experimental knowledge of God, issuing in service, ex-
pands in faith and love now that we know that God is
love who sent his Son to save us and abide with us in the
Eucharist and consequently in us by active presence.

The tests of being children of God and of abiding in
God are obedience (1 Jn 2:29, 3:24), love (4:7, 4:12), and
belief (5:1, 4:15) and are inseparably intertwined. Considering the human mind in its three functions of intellect, emotion, and will, we see that it is renewed in all
its parts by the indwelling of God: the intellect is enlightened to believe, the emotions are kindled to love,
and the will is turned and strengthened to obey.

"We can be sure that we know God only by keeping
his commandments" (1 Jn 2:3). This knowledge is faith
and involves conduct which is thus the criterion by
which we recognize life in Christ. Christians having
known the Son, the Son lives in them (1:3) and clothes

them in light, virtue, and love (1:7) and as this protects
us from the devil it constitutes our victory over him and
over this transient world through the power of God's
word which abides in us (2:13-14). This practical knowledge of God means a life lived in accordance with God's
revealed moral will. The high-sounding fellowship with
God has down-to-earth expression in obedience and that
to actual commandments. For John the knowledge of
God is not some vague, mystic vision or intellectual insight. It is shown if we keep God's commandments. Obedience is not a spectacular virtue, but it is at the basis
of all true Christian vision.

"Those who know God listen to us; those who are not
of God refuse to listen to us. This is how we can tell the
spirit of truth and the spirit of falsehood" (1 Jn 4:6). This
theme of the two spirits, which occurs also in the Qumran
literature, was destined to have a considerable influence
on early Christian thought. All people are torn between
two worlds and in varying degrees are all inspired by
the spirit of these worlds. For John the spirit of truth
comes from God and is communicated by the Christian
teachers.

"Everyone who loves is begotten of God and knows
God. Anyone who fails to love can never have known
God, because God is love. In this the love of God was
made manifest among us, that God sent his only Son
into the world, so that we might live through him" (1 Jn
4:7-8). The mission of the Son as savior of the world
manifests that love is from God, since God is love, and
enables the believer, God's son, to share in this love.
In the western world today it might be popular to equate
love with God, to see human love as something divine.
John rather means that loving is the most characteristic
activity of the Godhead, such love as was manifested at
the cross. God cares. This means more than God is loving. It means that God's essential nature is love. He loves,

so to speak, not because he finds objects worthy of his love, but because it is his nature to love. His love for us depends not on what we are, but on what he is. He loves us because he is that kind of a God. This doctrine is John's outstanding contribution to Christian theology. Of course, John's primary desire is to urge Christians to treat one another as God treats them, with gracious concern.

The motive of love is the origin of love in God: whoever loves thereby proves that he has his own origin in the same God with whom he has fellowship: He is born of God. Love not only comes from God as from a source, it is itself the very essence of God. It is this that deepens the sense in which it may be said that the one who loves knows God and is born of him. Christian love is not only a feeling of the force of natural affection or physical attraction or the warmth of friendship, but especially divine love. The divine begetting precedes that love; Christian love is an activity of the implanted eternal life, and is therefore a proof that the life is present. Such love can only blossom on the soil of Christian faith. The love of God was not attained by human endeavor; rather it was manifested in the life and death of the only-begotten Son of God, who gave us life and made a propitiation for our sins. Love of the brethren ought therefore to follow inevitably upon the recognition of the love of God manifested in the mission of his Son. If Jesus be denied or unconfessed, love is banished or unattained, but he who believes that Jesus is the Son of God abides in God and God in him, and love is the fruit of this indwelling.

Faith and love are the visible evidence of true union with God. God is in us Christians as the principle of our new life. Since God is light (1 Jn 1:5), virtue (2:29), and love (4:8, 16), whoever lives in union with God must live a life of light, virtue, and love, and keep God's commandments, especially the commandment to love one another. "God is light; there is no darkness in him at all. If we

say that we have fellowship with God while we are
walking in darkness, we lie and do not live according
to the truth. But if we walk in the light, as he is in the
light, we have fellowship with one another" (1 Jn 1:5-7).
We would expect the conclusion to say "fellowship with
him" but for John it was more important to remind
Christians that to profess love for the Father while
neglecting the Father's children, their own brethren,
is sheer hypocrisy. Religion without morality is an illu-
sion, just as morality has no foundation without religion.

Light is a natural symbol for attractive righteousness,
just as is darkness for the blackness of sin. Light is taken
first in a moral sense of holiness and purity, but it has
a rich complex of meaning. Light is outgoing and self-
communicating, and so light is the medium of fellowship
and love. Supremely it is God "who is in the light," the
Father and the Son in eternal, loving fellowship with the
Holy Spirit (2 Cor 13:13). Our fellowship with God finds
expression in fellowship with one another which has
already (1 Jn 1:3) been seen to be essentially the same
as fellowship with God. Christianity is not so much truth
to be believed as truth to be done because it is believed.
Religious experience which leaves human action un-
touched is thus shown to be false.

Walking is a metaphor for the whole way of life. It
is well adapted to bring out the truth that the Christian
should make steady, if unspectacular, progress. To walk
in the light is to live day by day with a strict care for
righteousness. There is to be no trifling with a low standard, as though all that matters is to attain a decent human
standard. The Christian is God's servant and he takes
his standards from God. He is to live in a God-like way.

Finally, the idea of abiding, living in God and of God
living in us is clearly an essential theme of John's Eucharistic doctrine (Jn 6:56-57). This fact receives added confirmation from the development of the concept in the

farewell discourses after the Last Supper (Jn 14:19, 15:4-5), our Lord's thanksgiving and prayer after the institution of the holy Eucharist.

16.

OUR DAILY BREAD

The Eucharist is the sacrament of the Paschal mystery, the mystery of our Lord's death and resurrection, and because our Lord is now the risen Christ, we might be tempted to gloss over his passion and death to focus all our attention on his blessed resurrection. Actually, we can never forget that our Christian life and its celebration in the Eucharist is essentially a participation in the death of our Lord, as we take up our Cross daily to follow him (Lk 9:23). Job's elegy on human frailty and misery (ch. 14), one of the great poems in all literature, underlines in all truth the stern realities of our human life, a truth we cannot afford to forget: "Man born of a woman has only a few days full of trouble." The Eucharist redeems and sanctifies our daily existence with its commonplace, routine, and mediocrity, its characteristic feelings of isolation and desolation, its slow death process, "prolixitas mortis," to quote St. Gregory the Great. The Eucharist is not only the climax of God's salvation history in the overall view, it is also the means of integrating our own personal spiritual history into God's total redeeming plan. The Eucharist is God's gift of personal salvation, the essential religious act of our life, our personal experience of God's saving pardon, our union with God as a foretaste of eternal life.

Our daily life is a world from which God seems very far; it is the domain of the profane and the secular, a world of business and pleasure but mostly of anxiety, pain, and suffering. Some people find little or no opposition between their daily experience of life and their own personal identity, so engrossed are they in secularity. Christians, however, feel torn apart by the contradiction they find between their daily life and the God they seek with all their heart. God's will, his love, his familiar presence, his grace, his pardon constantly risk being submerged by the cares and anxieties, the difficulties of their daily life. Life is really, with all its miseries, some kind of slow death. Its eternal monotony, its necessities, its vanity result in lack of interest, the dulling of our feelings, nervous fatigue, mental strain. Yet one could easily become completely absorbed in the mediocrity of one's daily life, especially when things go right, and lose contact with the real life which we call God.

There is evidently an abyss between our everyday life and the celebration of the Eucharist which is the summit of our salvation history, the reconciliation of mankind to God who makes himself available to us in the person of the Word made flesh. One is the domain of the sacred, proximity with God, the light of eternal life, eternal power, eternal glory, eternal victory over death, God's eternal wisdom, the infinity of God, limitless eternal life; the other is profaneness, estrangement from God, obscurity and misery, mediocrity, the sign of death. Yet the Eucharist itself, without losing its sacred, divine character, enables us to cross this apparently impassable chasm that separates us from God, by being our daily bread, the frame of our everyday life, the sacrament of our personal spiritual history of salvation.

Already the Council of Trent presents the Eucharist as our daily meal. "Christ gave us this sacrament as the spiritual food of our soul by which we are nourished and fortified by living his very life." "As I who am sent by the living Father, myself draw life from the Father, so whoever eats me will draw life from me" (Jn 6:57). Our

Lord is describing the chain of the sources of life, the bridge that enables us to reach eternal life. The life-imparting union between the Father and the Son is a figure of the life-imparting union between Christ and the believer. The believer's life, in fact, is intimately bound up with Christ's.

What is more daily than our meals? In this each day resembles the preceding one; we eat, we drink, we nourish ourselves. Such is the basic tissue of our daily life. And such is the Eucharist for us. It is our daily bread, the food that day by day nourishes our life and constantly builds up our strength. It is a meal that satisfies our constant need for food. It gives the strength feeble man needs every day to be renewed in his spiritual approach to God, and to grow in the love of God and of neighbor. Vatican II puts it this way: "The Lord left behind a pledge of hope and strength for life's journey in that sacrament of faith where natural elements refined by man are changed into his glorified body and blood, providing a meal of brotherly solidarity and a foretaste of the heavenly banquet" (GS, no. 38).

But there is more. Trent also says: "The Eucharist is the antidote which frees us from our daily faults and preserves us from mortal sin." Our daily life with all its miseries and human frailties, with our imperfections and weaknesses of character, finds in the Eucharist the remedy it needs to counteract the effects of original sin, the poison that infects the very structure of our human condition. The sacrament of life is also a preservative against serious sin, spiritual death. Vatican II also presents "the Eucharist as the source of perfecting the Church" (AG, no. 39).

Again according to Trent, the Eucharist is "the symbol of the one body whose head is Christ and to which Christ wanted us, as members, to be closely united by faith, hope, and charity, so that all of us might agree and that there be no dissensions among us (1 Cor 1:10)." This focuses on an important facet of our daily life since it is our destiny and duty to live with other people, as peaceably as possible. The heart of daily living is clearly to bear with one another, to help carry each other's burdens (Gal 6:2) in peace, patience, and love; to take it easy with our neighbor, to open the door of communication closed by misunderstanding or fear; to mix honesty with kindness, realism with forgiveness, toughness with sensitivity, trust with responsibility. According to Vatican II, "Truly partaking of the body of the Lord in the breaking of the Eucharistic bread, we are taken up into communion with him and with one another. Because the bread is one, we though many, are one body, all of us who partake of the one bread (1 Cor 10:17). In this way all of us are made members of Christ (1 Cor 12:27), but severally members one of another (Rm 12:5)" (GS, no. 7). "In his Church he instituted the wonderful sacrament of the Eucharist by which the unity of the Church is both signified and brought about" (UR, no. 2).

The Eucharist gives us the risen body of the Lord of glory but we cannot forget that he is always the Lamb of God, bearing even in his risen flesh the marks of his slaughter (Rv 5:6). The Eucharist is the memorial of the Crucified, of the death of Christ on the cross. His death has freed us from perdition; it is by his passion and death that he worked our redemption. Christ's destiny in instant, concentrated form is the cross, the mystery of Good Friday. All Christ's life had a saving value for us, but his death is clearly the climax, the utter manifestation of his love (Jn 13:1), of his dedication to the cause of human redemption. What was Good Friday for Jesus? An undiluted concentration of the miseries of our human existence: the absurdity of God being put to death by man, extreme suffering, betrayal and abandonment by his friends, oppression by the powerful people of this world. Good Friday was the day of absolute solitude, the day when was heard the incomprehensible and completely unexpected cry, "My God, my God, why have you abandoned me?" (Mt 27:46). Good Friday represents the vanity of life, the hatred of enemies, the betrayal of friends, black solitude, the absence of God, the expression of the stupidity of the princes of this world (1 Cor 2:8), and especially inexorable death. And is not all this what life is all about, the unadulterated essence of our daily life, what we constantly experience day in and day out? Already the ancient philosophers, like Seneca, saw life as the beginning of death, a thought taken up by Christian ascetic writers like St. Gregory for whom life is just death's delayed action **(prolixitas mortis),** a road that slowly but surely leads to the grave, a protracted death that we drink in drop by drop. If even "the paths of glory lead but to the grave," how much more the humdrum of our daily existence? A Christian is not a pessimist; for him life is not essentially evil; he can look up to life and recognize its worth, the joy and beauty it offers. But he also knows that life for itself is not worth living; that all is vanity (Ec 1:2), that without the risen Christ, we Christians are the most unfortunate of people (1 Cor 15:19). Life is a mixed blessing; it includes sickness, solitude, the silence of God, the fear of the future, the risks of chance and of the unpredictable and unavoidable, pain, sorrow, heartbreaking misery. Such is our human lot, our daily bread. And even if we do accept our daily experiences with a healthy good will which sees the hand of God and ignores any morbid self-pity, it remains true that looking at life in the face, one necessarily feels the weight and hardship of daily living, which does not diminish but increases as time goes by, underlining the crushing truth that life is a slow apprenticeship of death.

This situation, however, is not hopeless since the Eucharist is our daily bread, offering us the grace we need to live through our daily problems.

By the Eucharist, Jesus' saving action, his life and death penetrate into our own life, since the one to whom we unite ourselves is the Crucified; what we receive with the body of Christ is the very essence of our daily life, and day by day a foretaste, drop by drop, of our death and ultimate resurrection with Christ and in Christ. By receiving the Crucified, we receive each day, as the very soul of our life, the one who sends us out to our daily tasks. The Eucharistic celebration is the representation and the sacred sign of our Lord's death and cross which are the true dimensions of our own daily life. Each communion represents a profession of faith in the cross of Jesus. The glorious Lord who comes to us entered his glory by traveling the road of life that leads to the zero of death. This law of life which ruled our Lord's human existence, becomes our own as we share in his sacrament of life, because as St. Paul puts it, "As often as we eat this bread and drink the cup, we proclaim the Lord's death until he comes" (1 Cor 11:26).

The Eucharist is the grace of God operative in us to make our daily life part of Christ's life. Our life is not the result of chance but as in the case of Christ's human life, God's will for our salvation. When we receive the Eucharist, it is Christ's life that we receive and which becomes the interior law of our own life; and in this life, under the veil of faith, we discover a hidden life, a crucified life, a life leading to death, what we call daily living, the daily cross to which we are nailed after the example of Christ. It is hidden under the veil of mediocrity and of the commonplace, but receives from Christ who comes to us in the Eucharist, the strength, light, and grace, the daily bread we need to face up to our duty. Our daily life receives in him its meaning and is strengthened day by day with power, pardon, and holiness until we reach God's heavenly mountain.

How can we really make the Eucharist the sacrament of our daily existence, our daily bread? We must first gather up, as it were, our life in the center of our heart, realizing that there is God's home (Jn 14:23). Then in our inmost self we must have the courage to face up to ourselves and to the facts of daily living. Too easily we run from ourselves with all kinds of distractions, compensations, escapes. It is in the concrete of daily living that we must give ourselves to God by means especially of the theological virtues of faith, hope, and charity. To trust in God when fear, distress, anxiety, suffering crowd our life, is to accept our daily bread, exercising the holy virtues that have God as their object. This is how our Communions will effect in us their full purpose, as we pray to Christ: "Come, Lord, into my heart, you the Crucified who knows death, you in whom reside love, fidelity, truth, patience, humility; you who accepted a painful life, unreceived by your own, little loved by your friends, betrayed by them; you whose love went largely unrequited, you who took refuge in God and notwithstanding the fact that even he seemed to have abandoned you, gave yourself totally into his hands. I want to receive you as you are, I want to make you the interior law of my life, my life as it really is. It is from you that I learn its meaning and receive the strength to face it, this life, this little mound of ordinary events which nevertheless germs out an eternal life."

Our daily life should be the extension, the continuation of our Communion in our existential reality. The grace of the Eucharist is the strength that will lead us to accept our human condition, to remain always faithful to God in spite of temptation, to perform good works. But there is nothing grandiose or sensational in all this. We cannot expect that all our week days will be Sundays, red calendar days. As we receive our daily, ordinary life bread we should pray: "Help me, Lord, to handle, to endure my life today. Make it what it should be. I ache all over; my nerves are on edge; this day will be as usual full of aggravation, grey areas. Lord, stay with me. My daily life has nothing glorious or noteworthy, but it is your will that I want to do. Make it a continuation of what I am trying to do in Holy Communion. Stay close to me." Our daily life can thus become a communion. To continue in spite of failures and disillusions, to rise after a fall, to smile when things go wrong, to pray when one does not feel like doing so, to perform difficult or even revolting tasks, all this unites to God and leads to eternal life.

Thus our daily life is the maturation of our Communion, the digestion of our daily bread, but it is also the best preparation for our next holy Communion. The best way to prepare for holy Communion is to face victoriously the reality of each day, paying the price of such a victory. Our daily life, interpreted in a Christian spirit, leads us to Christ, the bread of our pilgrimage to God, our viaticum, our food for the road and even now the bread of eternal life.

17.

THE NEW COVENANT

There is no religion without worship but there is something new in Christian worship which sets it apart from all other religions. Already in the Old Testament preparation, the prophets had insisted that worship cannot be separated from a moral life. Witness the Israelites mentioned by Jeremiah. They thought they could steal, murder, commit adultery, perjure themselves and still present themselves to God's temple saying, "Now we are safe" (Jr 7:10). The prophet makes it clear that the temple is not a protection for evil doers; moral offences prove worship insincere. The sages in Israel also constantly make the point that there is no religion without morality: "The fear of Yahweh is the beginning of wisdom" (Pr 9:10). The fear of the Lord in the Bible is approximately what we call the virtue of religion, or devotion to God. Wisdom, the practice of virtue, or morality is its product; it finds in religion its principle and its crown (Si 1:18).

Jesus also is categoric that without the inward quality of genuine compassion, the exact performance of the law's external demands is hypocrisy. Twice (Mt 9:13, 12:7) he quotes the prophet Hosea's saying: "What I want is mercy not sacrifice" (Ho 6:6). Ceremonial religion is not set aside for to some degree ceremony must enter into man's worship of God. The quotation places human relations, moral duties, above positive institution, cultic worship.

Vatican II presents as "One of the gravest errors of

our time the dichotomy between the faith which many
profess and the practice of their daily lives" (GS, no. 43).
It also sees the Eucharist as "the summit toward which
the activity of the Church is directed, and as the source
from which all her powers flow" (SC, no. 10). "All the
other sacraments and all ecclesiastical ministries and
works of the apostolate are bound up with the Eucharist
and are directed toward it" (PO, no. 5). Christian worship
is then something very special, deeply different from
even the revealed religion of the Old Testament.

This appears first in the cultic terminology of the New
Testament. When referring to Christian worship the
sacred writers have avoided the use of the current terminology designating the worship of the Old Testament.
Such terms are used only for Christ, "the high priest"
(Heb 2:17) and indistinctly for all Christians who form
"a royal priesthood" (1 P 2:5). The Eucharistic worship
is given its own non-cultic terminology; it is "the breaking of the bread" (Ac 2:42), "the Lord's Supper" (1 Cor
11:23), and ultimately "the Eucharist" in the writings of
the Church Fathers.

What makes the originality of the New Testament
worship is its intimate relation to the Christian life, because it is the renewal of God's covenant with his people,
"the new and everlasting covenant" (Eucharistic Prayer),
which Christ in the Eucharist "established in his blood"
(1 Cor 11:25) (LG, no. 9). "The renewal in the Eucharist
of the covenant between the Lord and man, draws the
faithful and sets them aflame with Christ's insistent love"
(SC, no. 10).

The Eucharist is the new covenant predicted by Jeremiah (31:31-34). The essential characteristic of this new
covenant is that "Deep within them I will plant my Law,
writing it on their hearts. Then I will be their God and
they will be my people" (33). The new covenant is characterized by interiorization of religion; the law is no

longer to be merely a code regulating the external activity of man, but also, and especially, an inspiration working on his heart under the influence of the spirit of God who gives man a new heart. "I shall remove the heart of stone from your bodies and give you a heart of flesh instead. I shall put my spirit in you, and make you keep my laws and sincerely respect my ordinances" (Ezk 36: 26-27). The Holy Spirit will be the principle inspiring the new covenant. What is changed is not the content of the law, but its nature. It is not only something imposed from the outside but an interior principle of activity. It is written "not on stone tablets but on the tablets of your living hearts by the Spirit of the living God" (2 Cor 3:3), "the finger of God's right hand" according to tradition. The allusion is to the gift of the Law on tablets of stone on Mount Sinai (Ex 24:12) and to the prophecy of Ezechiel. The new relationship with God is personal and first hand, a spiritual bond. Those who are inspired by the Spirit of God not only know what God's commands are, but also possess the inward power to obey them. The result of the law written in men's heart, according to Jeremiah, will be that "they will all know me" (Jr 31:34). This knowledge of God is an assimilation and imitation of the divine character. God makes himself known to man when he engages himself to him by covenant and shows his love for him by the benefits he confers; similarly, man knows God when he loyally observes God's covenant, shows gratitude for God's gifts, and returns love for love.

This essential aspect of the renewal of God's covenant with man, which we find in the Eucharistic worship, is underlined by St. John both in Ch 6 when our Lord announces what will take place at the Last Supper, and in Ch 13 which gives the Johannine version of that event. For works in the Jewish sense, Jesus substitutes faith in God's messenger: "This is the work of God, that you

believe in him whom he has sent" (Jn 6:29). The essence
of religion is faith, the work most pleasing to God and
the foundation of all others. It is the work of God. Believing is not so much a work done by man as it is a
submission to God's work in Jesus. Faith is the highest
kind of work, for by it man gives himself; and a free-
being can do nothing greater than give himself. It is the
one work required because it is the solemn dedication of
the whole life to God and virtually includes in itself all
other works, and renders them acceptable.

St. Paul also speaks of the law of works as opposed
to "the law of faith" (Rm 3:28) which is "a faith made
operative by charity" as St. Thomas Aquinas puts it, a
living faith which consists in accepting the justifying
activity of God, a reception which is itself a gift of God,
and in giving this activity its full exercise in us. St. Paul
calls it also "the law of the Spirit of life in Christ Jesus"
(Rm 8:2), the law which is the activity of the Spirit in
us, as Jeremiah and Ezechiel had said. St. Paul adds
the precepts of the law, or rather the precept in the singu-
lar, since there is really only one in which all the others
are summarized: this is the precept of love "which is the
law in all its fullness" (Rm 13:10).

In St. John, Jesus explains that he will activate the
work of God in us by giving us a bread which unlike the
manna, really comes from heaven, "the true bread, the
bread of God" which the Father himself gives (Jn 6:32-
33). A bread which unlike the law (Si 24:21) will fully
satisfy: "He who comes to me will never be hungry" (Jn
6:35). Jesus continues, appealing to the prophets (Is
54:13, Jr 31:34): "It is written in the prophets: They will
all be taught by God" (Jn 6:45). Jesus clearly opposes the
covenant he came to establish with that struck on Mt.
Sinai. His covenant establishes immediate personal contact with God. Belief is not something a man can achieve
by his own unaided effort. It is acceptance of what God

puts directly into our mind and our heart. God teaches men in that he alone can utter his Word.

The Johannine Christ announces the gift that he will make of his flesh and blood for the life of the world (Jn 6:33, 51), opposing it more or less explicitly to the gift of the Law given by the intermediary of Moses in what constituted God's first covenant with the Jews. When the time came for Jesus to seal the new covenant with the holy Eucharist, John puts in bold relief what according to Jeremiah and Ezechiel is characteristic of the new covenant, namely, the gift of an interior law written in the heart of Christ's disciples, the law of Christian love!

It is by the mysterious presence of Christ in his disciples by the sacrament of the Eucharist that the new covenant announced by Jeremiah and Ezechiel is substituted for the old covenant. This mysterious presence, however, is not exclusively interior since it has its visible effect, the love that Christians have for one another, a love which is precisely the sign, the manifestation of the presence of Christ in our hearts. The gift of the new commandment after the washing of the disciples' feet, corresponds in St. John to the institution of the Eucharist in the Synoptics, as the sacrament of the new covenant in the blood of Jesus (Lk 22:20).

If the commandment is called new (Jn 13:34) it is by reference to the theme of the new covenant in the prophets. In fact, the newness of our Lord's commandment at the Last Supper is to be found not only in its content, as prescribing a greater love than the love demanded by the golden rule; it is more than a love by which we love our neighbor as Christ has loved us and not simply as we love ourselves. It is new not only in its motive, as a love given in the name of Christ's love. It is new especially in the very nature of the commandment which is not merely a norm exterior to ourselves but an interior principle of activity. There is more here than our Lord's approach in the Sermon on the Mount where Jesus commanded us to love even our enemies, but as Moses has ordered from the outside and merely by way of exhortation and example. At the Last Supper Jesus inscribes his commandment in the heart of his disciples; he communicates in a strict sense his life or more precisely his love at the very moment when this love reaches its uttermost consummation, its highest manifestation. "This is my commandment, that you love one another as I have loved you." And commenting on this new commandment Jesus continues: "Greater love has no man than this that a man lay down his life for his friends" (Jn 15:12-13). He loved us to the highest possibility of love and makes this love immediately available to us in the Eucharist, that we may enkindle its influence all around us.

St. Augustine and St. Thomas Aquinas have understood that the establishment of the new covenant is identified with the gift of the new commandment. St. Augustine commenting on Jn 13:34 states: "It is new because it strips us of the old man and clothes us with the new man, making us new men, heirs of the new covenant." St. Thomas is still clearer. "The new covenant is the covenant of the Holy Spirit because God's love for us has been poured out into our hearts by the Holy Spirit (Rm 5:5) and so the Holy Spirit effects in us the love which is the fullness of the law, and the new covenant not expressed by means of a written document, but by the very Spirit of God who is vivifying, the Spirit of life, according to St. Paul (Rm 8:2)." St. Thomas explains: "It is called the new commandment because of the renewal it effects in man by stripping the old man and clothing us with the new man, with the love that Christ demands of us. It is called new also because of the cause which produces it, namely, the Holy Spirit, the new spirit announced by Ezechiel. It is new, finally, because of the new covenant that it effects as Jeremiah had prophesied."

If the new covenant consists in the infusion of the Holy Spirit, and if the new commandment is the gift of this interior law, identified with the gift of the Spirit himself, it follows necessarily that the promulgation of the new commandment constitutes the new covenant. One can also see how in St. John the promulgation of the new commandment, the fruit of the Eucharist, corresponds to the Synoptic institution of the Holy Eucharist, which is the establishment of the new covenant.

The new commandment and the new covenant inaugurated by the sacrament of love are then closely related and practically identified. In St. John's mind, "I give you a new commandment" could well be the expression in other words of the same reality expressed by the Synoptic formula of the institution of the Eucharist, and would give some explanation of its omission in St. John's gospel. He had said with sufficient clarity in his chapter 6 that Christ's gift of himself would be through the sacramental medium of bread and wine: "the bread that I shall give is my flesh for the life of the world" (Jn 6:51). Later in chapter 13 he focuses on what is essential in what Jesus did at the Last Supper, the gift of his love, the effective sharing in his death and resurrection. That is precisely the meaning given by St. Paul to the words of the institution of the Eucharist which were already part of the Eucharistic celebration: "As often as you eat this bread and drink the cup, you proclaim the Lord's death until he comes" (1 Cor 11:26), a formula which was soon completed by the mention of Christ's resurrection, which was understood for St. Paul since for him Christ's death and resurrection constitute a single mystery, the Paschal mystery.

This idea of the indissoluble link between the gift of the Spirit and the Eucharist, the gift of love, the love of Christ for us and the love that we owe our neighbor, this is one of the aspects of Eucharistic worship most dear to the tradition, especially but not exclusively, of the oriental Church. The idea is underlined in the documents of Vatican II: "In the most blessed Eucharist is contained the whole spiritual good of the Church, namely, Christ himself, our Pasch and the living bread which gives life to men through his flesh, that flesh which is given life and gives life through the Holy Spirit. Thus men are invited and led to offer themselves, their works and all creation with Christ. For this reason the Eucharist appears as the source and the summit of all the preaching of the gospel" (PO, no. 5).

The introduction of the two epicleses in the new Eucharistic prayers gives liturgical expression to the same theological thought. "Let your Spirit come upon these gifts to make them holy, so that they may become for us the body and blood of our Lord Jesus Christ." "Grant that we who are nourished by his body and blood may be filled with his Holy Spirit and become one body, one Spirit in Christ." "May all of us who share in the body and blood of Christ be brought together in unity by the Holy Spirit."

18.

FRATERNAL COMMUNION

The promulgation of Christ's new commandment (Jn 13:34) is intimately related to the gift that our Lord makes of himself in the Eucharist, especially when we realize the practical identity of the Eucharist with the gift of the Holy Spirit viewed as a gift of love. This is the originality of Christian worship: its essential relation to practical human living. This is clearly how the first Christians understood the celebration of the Eucharist.

The Acts of the Apostles contain three composite editorial summaries (2:42-47, 4:32-35, 5:12-16) which paint similar pictures of life in the first Christian community in Jerusalem. Luke clearly intends to describe a community perfectly faithful to the teaching of Christ and docile to the inspirations of the Holy Spirit, or better still, a community animated by the Holy Spirit on Pentecost day. The second in which the prevailing idea is the pooling of resources, also follows immediately a second miniature Pentecost. This description of the life and activity of the Apostles, what they taught to their immediate disciples, is called the Apostolic Life **(Vita Apostolica)** by Tradition and is often referred to in the Vatican II texts. "The primitive Church provided an example of community life when the multitude of believers were of one heart and mind (Ac 4:32) and found nourishment in the teaching of the Gospel and in the sacred liturgy, especially the Eucharist. Let such a life continue in prayerfulness and a sharing of the same spirit" (Ac 2:42; PC no. 15). Four particulars are the test of a living Church: faithful ministry, constant fellowship, the due administration of the sacraments, and the observance of the appointed opportunities of prayer. These are the ideal facets of the first Christian community's life, not just its liturgical program.

In the first summary (Ac 2:41-47) the breaking of the bread occupies a significant place. The first Christians baptized after Pentecost "remained faithful to the teaching of the apostles, to fraternal communion **(koinonia)**, to the breaking of the bread, and to the prayers" (2:42). Among these four essential components of the Christian community only the last two refer directly to what we would call worship. The prayers which the author has in mind are not the private prayers which each one could perform in particular, but the official Jewish prayers which took place in the Jerusalem temple and in which the Christians still participated; in fact verse 46 states that "they went together to the Temple every day," and a little later we see Peter and John going up to the Temple for the prayers at the time of the evening sacrifice (3:1). Especially in focus must be the strictly Christian prayers presided over by the Apostles (4:24) within or outside the context of the Eucharistic meal.

The breaking of the bread describes the distinctive feature of early Christian worship, and could only be practiced in private houses since it was celebrated in the course of a meal, as Jesus had celebrated his Last Supper, and as was done in Paul's Corinthian community. The phrase suggests a Jewish meal at which the one who presides pronounces a blessing before dividing the bread.

Before mentioning the breaking of the bread, a quasi-technical name for the common meal which was the setting for the Eucharist, the Acts mention two other features of the ideal Christian community. The Eucharistic worship is at the heart of the Christian community but it supposes that certain previous conditions have been realized. The breaking of the bread is intimately related to the teaching of the Apostles and to fraternal communion **(koinonia)** which is given special prominence; it precedes immediately the breaking of the bread and thus appears as its special conditioning.

The celebration of the Eucharist demands a previous catechesis, all the more since it supposes an existing community. There is no strictly Christian community without faith in Christ and consequently without the preaching of Christ, since faith is born from hearing God's word (Rm 10:14). The point is underlined in the documents of Vatican II. "In the Christian community the preaching of the word is needed for the very administration of the sacraments. For these are sacraments of faith and faith is born of the Word and nourished by it. This is especially true in the liturgy of the word during the celebration of the Mass" (PO, no. 4).

There is question here of instructions for the newly converted in which the scriptures are explained in the light of the Christian event: the facts of the ministry, death, and resurrection of Christ as seen in the light of Old Testament prophecy. But the assimilation of this Christian doctrine, especially of what pertains to the Eucharistic mystery, is just a preliminary step for participation in Christian worship. A second condition, fraternal communion, is also indispensable and given special importance; the author of Acts, in fact, explains its meaning already here in the first summary (2:44-45) and consecrates to it practically all the second summary (4:32-35).

Koinonia, fellowship, is the fraternal communion which Christians must exercise in their every day life. St. Luke explains that "the faithful all lived together" (2:44); they formed a unity, not physical since they were about 3000 and broke the bread in their houses (46). They were a spiritual unity, a community. They had every-

thing in common (44). Their Christian fellowship was
expressed by concrete external manifestations. "They
sold their goods and possessions and shared the proceeds
among themselves according to what each one needed"
(45). This was an entirely free gesture since Barnabas is
praised for his generosity (4:38) and Ananias is punished
not for having refused to sell his field but for having lied
about the price obtained (5:4). When the text states, "No
one claimed for his own anything that he had, as everything they owned was held in common" (2:44), what is
asserted is that they considered their goods, whether
they sold them or kept possession of them, as destined for
the service of the community rather than for the benefit
and enjoyment of individuals. Vatican II basing itself on
St. Thomas gives the theology behind this practice. "In
using created things a man should regard his lawful possessions not merely as his own but also as common property, in the sense that they should accrue to the benefit
of not only himself but of others" (GS, no. 69). St. Thomas
explains that the owner of possessions should be ready
to share willingly with others in case they are in need.
This is the interior disposition supposed by the Acts. The
Christians shared willingly "according to what each one
needed" (2:45, 4:35). In these conditions it is inconceiv-
able that anyone could be in want, unless the whole community were in the same situation. That is exactly what
the text says: "None of their members was ever in want,"
as Dt 15:4 already demanded: "Let there be no poor
among you."

Fellowship, communion implies holding all goods in
common, thus expressing and reinforcing the union of
hearts which results from sharing the Gospel and all the
benefits received from God by Jesus Christ. It means
more than mutual social aid, common ideology, and a
sentiment of solidarity. It has its source, its foundation,
in the realities possessed in common, especially the spirit-

ual goods. The communion from which all the others derive, gives a share in strictly divine benefits: "God is faithful, by whom you were called into the fellowship of his Son, Jesus Christ our Lord" (1 Cor 1:9). It unites us to the Father and to his Son Jesus and to their Holy Spirit; it makes us children of God, sons with the Son. Because Christ shared our human nature, we are able to share in the divine nature. This fraternal communion became characteristic of the Christian community. It consists essentially in inner unity, in being of one heart and soul (Ac 4:32). The Christian sharing was an expression of the unity and harmony of the believers, manifesting their possession of the Spirit.

The type of life and character of the new community exhibited a movement of immense vitality and is best described as fellowship, a great sense of togetherness. They were so filled with the spirit of fellowship that they loved one another as truly as themselves. One of the most remarkable facts of the New Testament is the place which is assigned to charity of love (agape). And agape is the virtue of koinonia. It is not named in the Acts but it is exhibited in the whole life of the community not as a mere emotion, but as a sustained and practical activity. And it should be noted that in close connection with words and phrases that denote fellowship are terms that denote such attractive qualities as joy and gladness or again boldness, a glad fearlessness such as comes when men feel that they are at one with themselves, their fellows, and with God.

This fraternal communion is presented not only as one of the essential components of the Christian community but also as a condition of the breaking of the bread, the Christian worship. This worship demands that the faithful be instructed but also and much more that they strive to establish among themselves at all times, a true community, a family in which each one considers

and treats the other as "a dear brother", as St. Paul
says of the slave Onesimus (Phm 16). Fraternal communion and the breaking of the bread are very closely
related. Those who share in the Eucharist must be united
as they celebrate the sacrament, as the guests at a festive
meal, and manifest their union by and in the meal itself,
as was done in the primitive Church after the example
of our Lord, and as we still do by the giving of alms and
by the exchange of a peace greeting. But the link between fraternal communion and the breaking of the
bread implies in reality much more, even the transformation of all our life.

According to Vatican II, "The liturgy is the summit
toward which the activity of the Church is directed; at
the same time it is the fountain from which all her power
flows. For the goal of Apostolic works is that all who
are made sons of God by faith and baptism, should come
together to praise God in the midst of his Church, to
take part in her sacrifice and to eat the Lord's Supper.
The liturgy in its turn inspires the faithful to become
of one heart in love when they have tasted to their full
of the paschal mysteries; it prays that they may grasp
by deed what they hold by creed" (SC, no. 10).

The Council Fathers are referring to an ancient liturgical prayer used as post-communion in the Easter Vigil
Mass. "Lord, you have nourished us with your Easter
sacraments. Fill us with the Spirit of your love and make
us all one in heart (tua facias pietate concordes)." This
is a clear allusion to the description of the primitive
Christian community in Acts 4:32. We pray to be filled
with the Holy Spirit in which the Father loves the Son
and the Son his Father, and in which the Father and the
Son love all men, a love which is communicated to us
especially in the Eucharist, through the force of the new
commandment which it activates in us. We pray to be
established in perfect concord by sharing the piety which

is proper to God, that is, the care, zeal, and devotedness that he shows to us all, poor and needy. This merciful compassion, the fruit of the gift of God's love poured into our hearts by the Holy Spirit operative in the breaking of the bread, built up the apostolic community which remained faithful to the practice of fraternal communion.

The Constitution on the Church (LG, no. 28) states that priests, partakers of the mission of Christ, the sole mediator, "exercise this sacred function most of all in the Eucharistic liturgy or synaxis" (the Eucharistic assembly). The Council explains with a beautiful formula inspired by Cyprian, that one of the priest's first duties is to create this fraternal community. "Exercising within the limits of their authority the function of Christ as Shepherd and Head, they gather together God's family as a brotherhood all of one mind (Cyprian) and lead them in the Spirit, through Christ, to God the Father."

The Decree on the Ministry and Life of Priests also stresses the idea of the New Testament priest's responsibility as centering on building up the Christian community around the Eucharistic celebration and by means of it, "The Eucharistic Action is the very heartbeat of the assembly of the faithful over which the priest presides" (PO, no. 5). "No Christian community can be built unless it has its basis and center in the celebration of the most holy Eucharist. Here, therefore, all education in the spirit of community must originate. If this celebration is to be sincere and thorough, it must lead to various works of charity and mutual help, as well as to missionary activity and to different forms of Christian witness" (PO, no. 6).

This is the originality of the New Testament worship: its essential relation to daily Christian living. Eucharistic worship is an act of faith in Christ and in his love; but it is also an expression of love which directs the life of the Christian to the service of his brothers. It is especially a communication of Christ's love; it is the source from which Christian love flows, love for God with all that we are and have, and love for our neighbor as for ourselves and as Christ has loved us. The new commandment to love as Christ has loved is not engraved on stone or merely in the book of the gospels; Eucharistic worship consists precisely in impressing it deeply into the hearts of those who participate in spirit and in truth. The Christian minister of this worship is one who serves the community in a special way, according to the evangelical notion of authority (Jn 13:12-15).

Finally, the stone temple where the Old Testament worship was celebrated is replaced by the community itself, the body of the risen Christ (Jn 2:19-21). The Eucharistic worship can do without a temple edifice, but there is no celebration of the Eucharistic mystery possible without a community faithful to fraternal communion, the Church, of which the Eucharist is both the expression and the principle. The church structure is a symbol and an external and necessary help, but cannot take the place of an authentic community of fraternal communion.

19.

THE EVERLASTING COVENANT

Israel in its sacred history expressed its special relation with God by the idea of covenant. A covenant is an agreement between two parties by which both are mutually bound to do certain things on certain conditions and penalties. Such pacts between men appear frequently throughout the Old Testament. A suzerain and his vassal seal an alliance by a promise of protection from the lord and an oath of fealty from his subjects (Ezk 17:13). Israel used this experience to express the bond uniting them to God as his chosen people. The word covenant is used to express the relationship between Yahweh and the people of Israel; God's justice, his unchangeable nature, and his protecting power on the one side, and the corresponding duties devolving upon the people, especially as embodied in the law of Moses, on the other. The idea lies at the root of the whole conception of law among the Jews.

The covenant makes the life of Israel a dialogue with God but does not eliminate the inequality of the partners. It is not a bilateral contract between equals but an agreement between a superior and his inferior; the first imposes his will but his action is essentially a grace and an expression of liberality. In the covenant Yahweh imposes certain duties and in return promises to be Israel's God, to assist them and deliver them. The people accept their responsibility to God. For man the covenant is above all else an answer to the absolutely free initiative of God.

But obedience is more than a source of merit; it is a
thanksgiving, a recognition of what God was the first
to do.

The covenant is not a mere contract; it is essentially
a gracious act of God by which he binds himself to a
certain course of action in reference to the world or to
Israel, implying a bestowal of blessings and the revelation of his will. It establishes a close personal relationship
governed by God's covenant love **(hesed),** his loving kindness, his steadfast love, and by man's answer of self-
giving, loving trust, joyful submission to the will of God
and an active charity to his fellow men.

In the covenant of God with his people is summed
up the essence of the Old and the New Testaments, so
that, for example in Dn 11:28, "the holy covenant" comes
to mean the same thing as the religion of Israel. According to St. Irenaeus, "the glory of God is the living man".
Yet God who "created us without our co-operation will
not save us in spite of ourselves" as St. Augustine puts it.
Man is master of his own destiny but also responsible
before God. And God is ever ready to help us; in the
course of the history of our salvation he has "multiplied
his covenants with us" (Eucharistic Prayer IV). God
wishes to lead all men to a life of communion with him.
That is the idea behind the notion of covenant which
commands all the religious thought of both the Old and
the New Testaments, and will ultimately contain all the
mystery of Christ. A series of covenants make up our
biblical salvation history, especially five: the covenants
with Adam, Noah, Abraham, and Moses, and finally, the
new and everlasting covenant with, through, and in
Christ.

Deuteronomy 26:16-19 is notable as a declaration of
what God's covenant with Israel implies. "Yahweh your
God today commands you to observe these laws and cus-

toms; you must keep and observe them with all your heart and with all your soul. You have today made this declaration about Yahweh: that he will be your God, but only if you follow his ways, keep his statutes, his commandments, his ordinances, and listen to his voice. And Yahweh has today made this declaration about you: that you will be his very own people as he promised you, but only if you keep all his commandments; then for praise and renown and honor he will set you high above all the nations he has made, and you will be a people consecrated to Yahweh, as he promised." Yahweh is Israel's God whom they will obey; and Israel is God's people whom he will cherish and bless in a most special manner. The content of the covenant is summed up in the formula "you are my people, you are my God" (Ho 2:23).

The spiritual relationship between God and our first parents in Paradise is not called a covenant yet there is the equivalent of a covenant in Gn 1:28. God prepared the earth for man. If man lives up to God's expectation he will be "a fellow-worker with God" (1 Cor 3:9) and live up to his resemblance to God by the correct use of his intelligence and free will. Man is related to God by a spiritual bond, his likeness to God, from the very manner of his creation. His creation involves a covenant relationship. This relationship is far more than an impersonal Creator-creature relationship. The very creation of a reasonable and moral creature brought man into covenant with his God. The terms of the covenant are given in Gn 1:28: "God blessed them saying, 'Be fruitful, multiply, fill the earth and conquer it. Be master of the fish of the sea, the birds of heaven, and all living animals on earth'." The earth is God's gift to be put to profit and is itself the sign or memorial of the covenant. Man's honor is his task: to exercise dominion over the earth as God's representative (Ps 8). Procreation, in particular, is both

God's gift and his command, and man's task is to join in God's will for order. Man is assured of God's blessing in his responsibility of perpetuating the human race.

The story of man is also the story of broken agreements. From the beginning man proved prone to unfaithfulness to God. God recognizes as the status quo, fallen man in a disordered world (Gn 8:21) and pronounces his judgment upon corrupt and degenerate mankind by means of a destructive flood (Gn 6-9). The inspired author could only depict such a purely spiritual event as the breach in the relationship between God and man in symbolic terms. He shows the order established at the creation of the world breaking down in ruin. But God's purpose for blessing is undefeated and he begins to prepare the restoration which ultimately will be climaxed by the redemptive Incarnation.

The story of the Deluge is the vehicle for teaching eternal truths: God's righteousness, justice and mercy in his dealings with mankind; his holiness offended by moral evil; his stern punishment of sin; his abundant mercy in saving a remnant with whom he makes a new historical beginning, a righteous family in whom the divine purpose for men might be carried out. The flood is a divine judgment which foreshadows that of the latter days (Mt 24:37-38).

The particular teaching in the covenant with Noah is that of the uniform working of God in nature (Gn 8:22) and of his loving care for his creation. On these two ideas are based all physical science, which could not exist if there were no laws of nature, and all religion which would otherwise become mere superstitious dread of unseen powers. Noah's covenant appears as a new creation and repeats some of the features of the creation story. It secures the stability of the earth's conditions and of man's life. It includes again all mankind under divine promise and law. A new age opens with a renewal of the blessing which had been given at creation (Gn 9:1-2).

The sign of Noah's covenant is the rainbow (Gn 9:16). The ancients imagined the rainbow as God's weapon, his bow from which the lightnings of his arrows were shot. God places his weapon, his battle-bow in the heavens as a sign, a visible token that his wrath has abated. The sign is cosmic and reminds men that God's mercy will never be checked by man's sinfulness. It is a symbol, a memorial of the divine activity enthroned in everlasting mercy.

The third great stage in salvation history is marked by God's covenant with Abraham (Gn 17:1-11). This confirms the promise of the possession of the land of Canaan (Gn 15) and of a numerous progeny; it also lays down religious and moral obligations and gives circumcision as the sign of this covenant (Gn 17:11). Unlike the Noachian covenant, the Abrahamic "covenant in your flesh" (17:13) is binding on Israel only. God's covenant with man is getting more specific. Its purpose is to distinguish a new era in God's self-revealing witness to his people, an era which is signified by the change of Abraham's name as well as by the appropriation of new significance to an old rite.

Circumcision was originally a rite of initiation to marriage and to the life of the clan. It becomes a reminder for man of the obligations deriving from belonging to the chosen people. The shedding of the blood of that part upon which depends the perpetuation of life was the symbol of the continuous consecration of the nation to God from one generation to another. Circumcision is the ratification of the covenant by a symbolic act. It was a reminder of covenant obligations and a sign of membership in the covenant community. For Abraham it was a sign of his acceptance of God's covenant; at the time of the exile it was a sign of allegiance to Yahweh (Jr 9:25-26). St. Paul explains it as "the seal of the righteousness of faith" (Rm 4:11). The Fathers have seen it as an antitype of Christian baptism.

The Mosaic covenant is brought down to the level of the people. By the terms of this covenant the Israelites become Yahweh's special possession out of all the peoples of the earth, a holy nation (Ex 19:5). The covenant is ratified with the sprinkling of the blood of victims and with a communal meal (Ex 24:1-21). The conditions of the covenant are the ten words of Yahweh, the Decalogue (Ex 21:1-17). Under Moses the covenant brings with it the obligation of fidelity to the law (Ex 19:5, 24:7-8) and to the Sabbath observance in particular (Ex 31:16-17). The Sabbath is the sign for ever of the Mosaic covenant (Ex 31:16). The separation of one day in seven is a symbol of the separation of the entire people, of its consecration to God; it is the perpetual memorial of the agreement between them and Yahweh who sanctifies them.

Moses is the mediator between God and man; he unites them symbolically by sprinkling the blood of the same victim first on the altar, which represents Yahweh, and then on the people. In this way the pact is ratified by blood which is considered as the life-principle, just as the new covenant is ratified by the blood of Christ. In the Eucharistic continuation of Christ's sacrifice it is in the consecration of the chalice that this character is emphasized.

Isaiah describes the Servant of Yahweh as "the Covenant of the people" (42:6), the bond, the mediator uniting them to God, the embodiment of a new covenant. It is through him that God will make himself known and communicate his final revelation. This was fully realized in Jesus who, in his own person, united the Lord and his people. By shedding his blood on the Cross, Jesus fulfilled the covenant sealed on Mt. Sinai by the blood of sacrifice (Ex 24:4-8); he also announced implicitly that the new covenant predicted by the prophets (Jr 31:31-34) is accomplished. The blood of Jesus, his sacrifice inaugurates the final days of the history of man's salvation; in his progressive self-revelation God enters into a constantly more intimate personal relationship with man which culminates in the Eucharist in its most exalted and immanent form.

Jesus not only strikes, concludes the new covenant, he himself is the covenant. His being which unites his divinity and his humanity in the unity of one person, is the source from which his mission flows; he is universal reconciliation because he unites in his body the dust from which the human race was fashioned, and the gold, the glory of the divinity. Likewise he seals the covenant between God and mankind because he unites humanity and the divinity in his person; his body is the dwelling place of love especially in the Eucharist where man finds intimacy with God and at the same time peace with his neighbor. The Eucharist is the sacred bond that unites all believers with each other and with their glorified Lord. A significant point about the participles "given" and "poured out" in the Eucharistic texts is that they indicate the divine and the human aspects of Christ's covenant action in the Eucharist. In so far as he is giving himself to his Apostles he is acting as the divine initiator of the new covenant with men; in so far as he gives himself as vicarious victim for the redemption of man, he is acting above all as a priestly mediator, and this giving of himself for his brethren is at the same time a sacrificial gift to his Father, a perfect compliance with the Father's will to redeem mankind.

The Eucharistic action of Jesus continues and fulfills the whole Old Testament history that was dominated by the idea of covenant. It is a covenant meal in the fullest sense, for God is actually sharing his divine life with us;

it is not only commemorative, for it is the continued presence of Christ who is the concrete embodiment and realization of that relation between God and man which is the covenant, and it is the continued enactment of that action by which Christ constitutes the new covenant.

Jesus is the new covenant; he is its source, its recipient, and its mediator. He is Emmanuel, the covenant presence of God with men; he is the supreme attachment of man to God; and this devotedness to the Father's will finds its full actuation in his sacrificial self-offering at the Last Supper.

The covenantal action of Christ in the Eucharist is not static but dynamic. The relationship between God and man is not simply a relationship consequent upon the salvific action of Christ; it is a continued mediation by Christ, an active relating of God to men and of men to God effected sacramentally in the Eucharist. In this context the truth of Christ's real presence in the Eucharist is not only logical but the only thing that gives full meaning and actuality to the new covenant dispensation that is Christianity. Jesus replaces the Temple as the center of true cult; henceforth it is in and with him that men will encounter and worship God. Jesus constitutes a new chosen people whose religious life will be centered around and spring from the covenant meal and who will find communion with God and with one another in Jesus' unique sacrifice made effective in the life of the Church each time we celebrate the Eucharist.

Jesus himself at the Last Supper is the last sign of God giving himself in the most thorough and free way imaginable. The sign of the cross is God's sign par excellence; not because of the suffering and death it entails but because of the gift it manifests (Jn 3:15). And it is memorialized in the Eucharist which is not only an empty remembrance of it but its recall, the possibility of communion with the gift itself: the gift of Christ crucified

but risen again in glory and seated at God's right. God
has never finished giving himself because the paschal
mystery remains actual until the end of time.

The role of the meal is to nourish but also to reunite.
A banquet is the normal climax of a treaty, pact, or festival. The Eucharist proclaims to the world and for all time
liberation from all slavery, dignity, liberty, justice for all.
The total gift of the Son of God, it is the absolute and
definitive sign of life, the very life of God himself. The
Eucharist is not a mere fraternal meal, a mere symbol
of understanding and affection; it is meant to transform
all our human existence. It serves God's project for hu-
manizing man, helping him live a successful human life
and achieve spiritual harmony. The glory of God is the
living man!

The Eucharist is the life of Christ given to me so that
I may live like Christ. It is the source where one will
find the strength for the combat of human living. The
Christian must be a prolongation of the Incarnation of
Christ by continuing his struggle for justice and peace.
He must nourish his brother with his own substance so
that they may live because of him. The passion of Jesus
will last till the end of the world, and by the Eucharist I
take it into my own life and assume my share of God's
redemptive plan and consequently a piece also of Christ's
transfiguration and ultimately of his resurrection. The
Eucharist teaches us that the gift of ourselves does not
lead to annihilation but to fulfillment. The Church, the
body of Christ, is born in human birth pangs and each
member's contribution helps to realize God's plan in the
creation and recreation of humanity.

20.

LITURGICAL WORSHIP AND PERSONAL PRAYER

Liturgical worship and personal prayer both depend upon and refresh one another. According to Origen (On Prayer, 33) the basic forms of Christian praise and prayer are systematized as adoration, thanksgiving, confession, and petition, including intercession. Now both styles, liturgical and personal worship, need the balance of adoration, thanksgiving, confession, and petition that comes from hearing and meditating upon the word of God, and both require that dedication of commitment to discipleship congruent with being members one of another in the one Body of Christ.

Two normative foci of Christian spirituality are corporate worship with one's fellow believers, and private prayer and meditation. Moreover a most necessary and especially rewarding expression of Christian living is found in the gospel works of mercy, feeding the hungry, clothing the naked, and visiting the sick and prisoners (Mt 25:35-36). All these approaches to Christianity, public worship, private prayer, social engagement, must exist side by side in the different individuals in varying degrees of intensity. But the works of beneficence must be done in view of Christ: "You did it to me . . . you neglected to do it to me," (Mt 25:40, 45). And without these works, corporate worship is sterile and routine, and personal piety is empty of meaning.

Some people sincerely believe that public worship interferes with true worship of God. They assume that

God must be known in an experience so private that the
throng of human souls crowded together in one small
place removes God from the scene in ratio to the number
of persons so gathered. Yet public worship and private
devotion should be mutually supportive. Public worship
makes significant contributions to the practice of private
devotions, and private devotions have their own bene-
faction for meaningful public worship. The solitary worshiper who prefers his solitude risks a self-centered faith
in his icy segregation from others. His love of God, which
is what worship is all about, his professed love is quite
questionable. St. John says: "A man who does not love
the brother that he can see cannot love God, whom he
has never seen" (1 Jn 4:20). Love of God is shown by
love of man. If one is lacking so is the other. To affirm
one's love for the unseen while failing to love the seen
is to enter the realm of fantasy. Love to God as a mystical emotion is meaningless unless the reality of this love
is shown by loving God's other children, our brothers.
Public worship reminds us that God has business with
all people, and not just with special individuals who
imagine they have an inside track to God, or some privileged private line of communication.

Religion consists essentially in learning about God.
Now the most direct instruction about God comes in the
reading and explaining of the Scriptures. According to
St. Ambrose: "We speak to God when we pray; we hear
him when we read the divine sayings." The most con-
sistent and comprehensive explanation of what is read
from the Bible can be expected to be received in the
assembled community. Little Bible reading and study
take place without the basic instruction of the Church
at worship. God is best known when the worshiper hears
about him in the context of public worship.

Words are not the only means by which the worshiper
learns about God. The actions of the gathered commun-

ity also communicate a message. The Lord's Supper in a
special way silently speaks of God, teaching of his continuing mercies, of his presence among his people, and
of the hope of Christ's triumphant return. As we come
to the place of worship, we recognize a place hallowed
as a place where one meets God. The friendly greetings
at the door by fellow-worshippers convey something of
the warmth and meaning of Christian fellowship. The
act of standing together, kneeling together, bowing the
head together, or of making the sign of the cross together,
teaches of a unity of all men in need and in faith before
God.

Worshiping with others is a means of relating cre-
atively to the community of believers. Public worship
opens certain doors to brotherly charity, community concern, and world service, which may remain closed to the
person who worships only in private. When believers pray
together they discover their mutual needs and bear their
mutual burdens. They get a vision of tasks that require
their joint action. When Christians are deprived of the
opportunity of public worship, for example, in time of
persecution, they realize as never before their need for
it. This worship may be taken half-heartedly as long as
it remains an option, but when it becomes no longer
possible, one may feel as the psalmist in his exile from
Jerusalem and the Temple: "As a doe longs for running
streams, so longs my soul for you, my God. My soul
thirsts for God, the God of my life; when shall I go to
see the face of God?" (Ps 42:1). The psalmist gives expression to his love for the Temple and for God's presence
there. His sorrow arises from his inability to get to Jerusalem where alone the living God may properly be worshiped. Vatican II says the same thing in its own way:
"Day by day the liturgy builds up those within the
Church into the Lord's holy temple, into a spiritual
dwelling for God (Ep 2:21-22), an enterprise which will

continue until Christ's full stature is achieved" (Ep 4:13)
(SC, no. 3).

All this implies that public worship is a means of
rendering service to the world as well as to God. In fact
two main tasks occupy the Church, intercession and getting God's work done in the world. Intercession is an
essential part of general public worship. No petition is
too humble to be a part of this corporate concern. Worship begins with Jesus Christ, flows through the life and
influence of the believers and finds its goal in the world.
The Church extends God's purpose through its action.
What the Church agrees to do becomes, if the Holy Spirit
is followed, God's service to the community, ranging all
the way from almsgiving to foreign missions.

Public worship protects private devotion. It forestalls
its disuse by overflowing into the pensive hours of our
solitude, leading to individual practice of adoration,
thanksgiving, confession, intercession, supplication, and
dedication. One who prays the Lord's prayer with his
Christian brothers each Sunday will at least occasionally
remember its meaning in the small and great crises that
develop between Sundays.

Also, public worship protects private devotion from
misuse. Private prayer can be self-centered, self-congrat-
ulating, and self-seeking. But if it is, it must be so against
the stream of what corporate prayer teaches. In private
prayer I may be tempted to seek only my own success,
but in corporate prayer I am reminded of the claims of
the kingdom of God. Left to myself, if I do not eventually
leave off praying altogether, I am likely to make prayer
an extension of the unregenerate part of myself, rather
than the part of me that finds fulfillment in the larger
interests of God and my fellow man.

Prayer, whether public or private, is a desire to receive God within ourselves, to unite ourselves to him;
it is at the same time a waiting, an expectation, a seeking,

an aspiration. Since it is the most personal thing in the world, prayer admits of as many forms as there are souls in the Church. As there are no two identical souls, there are no two identical prayers. God's love toward each one of us is personal and unique; and our love for him should have the same character of intimacy. On the other hand, we are part of a divine society, a body, Christ's Mystical Body. Consequently, our prayer is unavoidably a prayer of the Church; a prayer in and with the Church. This is one of the mysteries involved in prayer. Prayer is personal and unique, the most personal and unique reality we could imagine. And still at the same time prayer is never really a solitary posture in the presence of God. As Martin Buber puts it, in our I-Thou relationship with God we normally find the Thou of God in the thou of man. Buber had in mind the beneficence which one must exercise towards his neighbor. But the reality goes further. All our brothers in the Church pray in us, with us, and for us. We pray in them, with them, and for them. This kind of antimony between the personal and universal aspects of prayer is a great mystery, a mystery of faith. Prayer is our acceptance of God, an assent given to God and his mysteries, an assent to everything God does for us, an assent to his work of salvation. The object of Christian prayer is the fullness of salvation. Now our salvation has been accomplished in the sacrifice of Christ, a sacrifice operative in the Eucharist. Therefore all Christian prayer is Eucharistic. All prayer is directed to the Eucharist, receives its value from the Eucharist, has its summit, explanation, and perfect realization in the Eucharistic celebration and in holy Communion.

Because it is simple, prayer embraces the whole Christian posture, the whole Christian bearing. There is an infinite diversity in prayer: because each soul is unique, each grace, which is our individual sharing of God's love, is different. Nevertheless, there is a marvelous **unity** in

the essence of prayer, as much as in its different forms.
The same Spirit of Christ prays in all of us. We all receive in our own personal way the same salvation, which
is available to all of us above all in the Eucharist, the
focus of all the other sacraments and other means of
grace. The basic form of prayer is also one. If we consider
the traditional doctrine of prayer, we shall see that the
unity of the different forms and expressions of prayer
flows from the fact that prayer to God must be expressed
above all in God's own words. And since God has spoken
to us in the Bible, the Holy Scriptures must be the normal
source and fountain of prayer. Moreover, Christ being the
Word of God Incarnate, he is the main subject matter of
God's revelation, and the summary of all Christ's teaching
is found in the Eucharistic words over the bread and
wine, "Do this in memory of me."

The Bible, God's revelation, is the source of the unity
of the two traditional forms of prayer: liturgy and meditation. There is no liturgy without Scripture, nor is there
any meditation without the Bible. Liturgy is the Church's
celebration of the mysteries of Christ, the principal one
being his Passover, the mystery of his death and resurrection. The other mysteries prepare for it, continue it, or
reveal its contents, its consequences, its richness to us.
The liturgical celebration of the Eucharist is itself a mystery beyond human words. And it is precisely because of
this that the liturgy is mostly biblical, inspired by the
Bible or taken from it. The only way we can speak to God
is with his own words, to elevate us and raise us beyond
ourselves. The Mass is, through the texts of the liturgical
cycle, an illustration of the mystery of Christ which is
realized in the Eucharist, made available to all believers
day by day. The liturgy is meditative prayer. What we
need is not so much to understand as to share. Our meditative prayer consists in sharing, assimilating the mystery of God proclaimed in the words of the Bible. In the

liturgy we disappear behind prayer, the Church, and the words of God. God is the principal author in the liturgy; it only remains for us to say, "Yes, Amen," only to sing "Alleluia, Praise God", as the saints do in heaven, according to the book of Revelation (19:4).

What would the liturgy be without the Bible? Either it would not exist at all, or it would be reduced to a simple collection of pious devotional practices. These would certainly be easier to understand, but also surely less nourishing for the spirit; marked, besides, with the imprint of one era or one man, and bereft of that universal character of the great Catholic liturgies which focus around what the God-man, Jesus Christ, said and did. We can also think of what the Bible would be without the liturgy. It would not be that living book, that living teaching, that substantial food which the Church gives us in the Blessed Eucharist. We would hear some pages read from a book, but it could not be a living reading since there would be no action, no sacraments, no reality, because there is no liturgy.

St. Benedict in his holy Rule gives this advice: "Let our mind and our voice be in harmony." In the liturgy we are invited to harmonize our spirit with what the Church does through us in speaking to the Lord. The liturgy is meditative prayer, since it consists in placing our heart, our spirit, our entire soul, and our body, in harmony with the words our mouth pronounces, God's own words. In the same way, according to tradition, meditation essentially consists in placing our human spirit in harmony with God's revelation contained in God's inspired word, the holy Scriptures. The essential is not the words, but the attitude and acceptance, the presence of God in the one who prays. We have to accept the mystery of salvation with our whole being; and in our human condition, the Eucharist is its perfect fulfillment. It is the heart of both liturgical and personal prayer.

Actually, the Eucharistic celebration is neither an individual prayer, nor a collective prayer, but the prayer of Christ himself. It is not the repetition of a prayer made at some past time by Christ, but the prayer of the living Christ today, his perpetual intercession for us "since he is living forever to intercede for all who come to God through him" (Heb 7:25). As the body of Christ, we must share in his prayer, to be incorporated to Christ and be one with him before God. My personal prayerful effort remains my particular contribution but it forms part of the community of the faithful people of God, of whom Christ is the head.

Prayer is then not so much a dialogue with God, but rather a duet with Christ in God's honor, or better still a trio which includes our neighbor and consequently develops into a full orchestra under the leadership and direction of Christ. Prayer does not consist merely in stating problems and receiving answers, but rather in placing our voice in harmony with the voice of God in the Church and in ourselves, in harmonizing our voice with that of Christ and of our fellow Christians. These are the three strands that make prayer so powerful: "A threefold cord is not quickly broken" (Ec 4:12).

21.

THE EUCHARIST, YESTERDAY, TODAY, TOMORROW

Until recently a treatment of the Eucharist would insist that the sacrament of the altar reproduces, without repeating it, the sacrifice of the cross, for our salvation, because it contains really the body and blood of Christ. This thinking is not, of course, obsolete, yet theologians today feel the need of insisting on the spiritual theology of the sacraments and their ethical context, their relation to moral action, motive, or character. For the Eucharist this means insistence on the meal character of the sacrament and its influence on the Christian life. Each period has its own needs, and it is always profitable to take into account new developments without discarding, of course, what was durable in the traditional approach.

Attending Sunday Mass and receiving Holy Communion at least at Easter time still remain a real witness to one's Christian faith, but such practices are clearly minimal and need further development and deepening. It would be wrong, however, to neglect acts of devotion to the Eucharist, in the form of preparation for, and thanksgiving after Holy Communion, and prayerful visits to the Blessed Sacrament, on the pretext of focusing on the essential Eucharistic celebration, or again because some might have cultivated an excessively dolorous approach to these pious acts, for example, in the form of self-righteous acts of reparation to the Prisoner of Love. Witness Charles de Foucauld and his Little Brothers and

Sisters, and Mother Teresa: prayer before the Blessed
Sacrament, as a complement to the Eucharistic celebration, is still a source of spiritual strength for the most
apostolically-minded Christians.

There is some appeal to Teilhard de Chardin's vision
of the Eucharist as the Mass over the world, a sun trans-
forming the world by the progressive transfiguration of
matter and humanity to the likeness of Jesus Christ. Less
romantic and more realistic is the theology of work and
of the consecration of the world, which sees the Eucharist
as the work of human hands and the Mass less as the
transmutation of a substance, calling for admiration of
such a prodigy, and more as the building up of the Body
of Christ. The Eucharist is a promise and a ferment as
well as a memorial; like the Passover, it is celebrated as
the community feast that it always was meant to be.
The Eucharist is seen today in closer relation to the three
spheres of our modern society: the family, the economy,
the city. The Eucharist effects a loving union, it demands
hard work, and calls for a difficult reconciliation, that is,
civic understanding and living together.

Much in vogue also today is a focusing on personal
liberty and on the importance of conscience. Yet we are
well warned against an egoism which is as self-destructive as it is opposed to the purpose of the Eucharist; and
against subjectivism, for example, in the understanding
of the real presence of Christ in the Eucharist as a mere
interpretation of the believer's faith.. Secularity, man's
satisfaction with himself in his world, also comes into
the scene. The danger here is greater, especially if man
loses all interest in the sacred. The Eucharist could degenerate into some kind of fraternal cocktail party where
the memorial of Christ's passion is obscured in songs of
earthly joys. Then there is the theology of liberation
invoked in favor of the third-world. Here also the Eucha-

rist has a clear role to play, seen already by St. Paul a long time ago, when he told the Corinthians (1 Cor 11:17-34) that their Eucharist was a comedy unless the richer members of the community shared their food with their poorer brethren. Finally, whereas just a short while ago, our young people, especially, experienced an allergy to prayer, the tendency right now is again in favor of different forms of prayer, charismatic, communitarian, and before the Blessed Sacrament as proposed in the introduction to the new Sacramentary.

St. Paul refers to God's plan for our salvation as the mystery of God (Rm 16:25). That is the key word from the beginning for the Christian rites which give us access to the love of the Father by incorporation with his Incarnate Son in the Holy Spirit. Soon, however, the word sacrament took over but in the ancient sense of the fealty oath or pledge of allegiance. The sacrament is then understood as our thing, ordained to our personal sanctification, which it is, but it is above all God's gratuitous gift. And insistence on the subjective character of the sacramental rite could build up such a wall between God and man that the secularist could come to prefer his own interior conviction and freedom to a desacralized religious rite.

With St. Augustine the sacrament is understood as an effective sign of invisible divine grace, but granting that revelation puts us in contact with the unapproachable, the fact remains that it is in Christ that we find God and not behind him. Christ has life in himself (Jn 5:26) and remains personally available to us in the sacraments, especially in the Eucharist. Glory is not hidden behind the cross; it radiates from the crucified. Or as St. John puts it (Rv 5:6) the lamb of God is presented to our adoration with the marks of his slaughter still fresh in his risen body. We are invited to lift up our hearts to

God but especially to enjoy heart to heart relations with
Christ (Rv 3:20). We must believe in God but love is the
purpose of it all.

The theology of the word of God as contained in Holy
Scripture is receiving the attention it deserves, since
our faith is nourished from preaching the word about
Christ (Rm 10:17). The word of God and the Holy Eucharist are closely related. In fact, God's message is Christ,
the Incarnation, a message of flesh and blood. Without
the body of Christ there is neither Eucharist nor Scripture, in fact no revelation. As St. Augustine puts it, the
word is spoken over the elements and the result is the
sacrament. The Eucharist is not a thing or an idea but
the very body of Christ. God does what he says. The word
consecrates the bread, but it is the consecrated bread that
gives meaning to the word, not only of consecration but
to every word God has ever spoken. Christ's Eucharistic
words are an invitation not only to listen, to take and eat,
but also to assimilate in the silent prayer of contemplation.

The theology of liberation has taken unwarranted
liberties. Focusing on the universal priesthood of the
faithful (1 P 2:9) has brought about a devaluation of the
ministerial priesthood, if not an attempt to evacuate it.
Theology and philosophy are also too easily relegated
to the background, if not totally ignored; "ideas divide"
becomes a popular slogan. Consequently conscience and
practical conduct are canonized, a situation which evidently leaves no place for the sacraments, or even for the
Church. Conscience, however, must be enlightened. As
the Old Testament had already pointed out, there is no
solid morality possible without religion (Pr 1:7), and true
religion cannot make abstraction of the temple which is
Christ's body (Jn 2:21) and of those whom he has chosen
as his representatives (Jn 17:18).

Not so long ago uniformity was the cry of the day;

any particular approach could be suspected as being contrary to tradition. Now pluriformity is in style. The many-
splendored mystery of the Eucharist here again has no
problem of accommodation to any legitimate approach
to the mystery of Christ. For example, for the average
person a sign is something quite banal, lacking in character or substance. Like the symbol it denotes something
opposed to the real or effective. To speak of symbol for
Christ or the Eucharist would seem a departure from the
true faith. Yet the term is quite orthodox. Three times
the Council of Trent uses it saying that, "Our Savior left
the Eucharist as a symbol of unity and charity"; that this
sacrament is "the symbol of a sacred reality and the
visible form of an invisible grace," "the symbol of concord". The symbol is simply what puts two things together, the reality involved in this union being gaged
by the nature and the results of the union itself. The
sign or symbol always means something but what is
meant by a symbol created by the Holy Spirit must be
unusually rich in significance. In the Eucharist two realities of different order come together under the symbol,
human nourishment and the body of Christ. Our Lord
gives himself to us in truth but under the symbol of
bread and wine.

The sacrament supposes first the absence of Christ,
his death, resurrection, and return to the Father. It replaces the earthly presence of Christ during his mortal
life, but he has not left us orphans: we have been weaned
but not abandoned. Christ is still present to his Church,
especially in the Eucharist, a presence which is not merely spiritual, since it is the presence of a body, risen it is
true, but not a pure spirit. In fact, the Eucharist is impossible unless there is a resurrection of the body to be
given as our spiritual food. The sign of food would have
no value, if there were nothing to eat. It is by faith that
we eat but faith does not create its nourishment, it re-

ceives it. The sacramental symbol is not arbitrary since there is a link between the nourishment of our soul and the bread which is chosen as its sign. But it is not natural either since the bread is transfigured as is the body of Christ. By the intervention of the Holy Spirit, it acquires a real super-value which is known by faith in the words of the Lord, a faith that is beyond, not contrary to, ordinary human experience.

The Eucharist is first of all the satisfaction of our need for God's grace. Taking food is the acknowledgement of an elementary need for growth through nourishment. The Eucharist meets this need in the supernatural order. The Eucharist satisfies the four basic needs of a human being, for truth, beauty, goodness and unity, the so-called transcendentals. Different historical periods have reacted differently to these needs in relation to the Eucharist.

At the beginning of the Middle Ages, insistence was on the truth of the Eucharist, because of the controversies about Christ's presence in the Blessed Sacrament. This is the true body of Christ, born of the Virgin Mary, we still like to sing (**Ave verum corpus**), seeking to establish a link between the present and the past. The ecclesial, unity aspect of the sacrament, however, should not be glossed over or neglected. The late Middle Ages were especially sensitive to the beautiful, and produced the baroque extravaganza in church decoration, with the exaggerated desire of seeing the consecrated host. This style is now obsolete but not the need for contemplative Eucharistic prayer which is something else. The believer knows that the Eucharistic bread is meant first of all to be eaten, but he still wants to contemplate and venerate the humble elements that bring him his Lord. This desire is perfectly respectable and legitimate, provided it remains in the sacramental limits and avoids irrelevant or questionable considerations.

The goodness of the Eucharist has also been underlined. Holy Communion is a joy, a transfusion of holiness
that should bear fruits in our life. There is intimate joy
in being united to Christ, in having him as our companion
on the road of life; our courage is bolstered by the certitude that nothing can really separate us from his love
(Rm 8:35), that through the grace of the sacrament we
have an antidote against temptation. Emotionalism here
would be the danger or sentimentalism, instead of humble appreciation of the privileged moments of prayerful
contemplation possible by God's love manifested in the
Eucharist; the "unbelievable familiarity" mentioned in
The Imitation of Christ.

Much insistence is given today to fraternal and ecclesial unity as a fruit of the Eucharist. This again is all to
the good provided that this fraternal love rises above the
horizontal level and is not a mere celebration of human
fellowship. It is the host that gives me a Christian heart
to cherish my brother as God does. Communion gives
me the Lord as food, so that my charity may become my
brother's food. The precept of love is indivisible, but the
union of our human hearts can only be accomplished by
the acceptance of God's grace.

Finally, the Eucharist is the meaningful union of all
the mystery of Jesus: his life, his resurrection, and his
return. This fact appears clearly in St. John, especially
in his chapter six. He describes salvation as a double
movement of descending-ascending or entering-going out.
Descending (Jn 6:32, 51) and entering (Heb 10:5) describe
the Incarnation, symbolized by the bread which comes
from heaven and is the body of Christ. Ascending (Jn
6:62) and going out (Jn 13:3, Lk 9:31) stand for the Passion
and the glorious Resurrection and Ascension to God's
right. For John the Last Supper is the grand union of
Christ's coming on earth and of his return to the Father:
"I came from the Father and have come into the world

and now I leave the world to go to the Father" (Jn 16:28).
Body and blood signify the totality of his human life;
bread and wine, eating and drinking, signify the totality
of nourishment and nutrition. The liturgical year is thus
well-organized around the two poles of Christmas and
Easter-Pentecost, the foretaste of eschatology. The Mass
is a sacramental Pentecost, each Eucharistic celebration
being a sort of spiritual relay on the long road that leads
to the Parousia, the consummation of God's kingdom.

Such is the Eucharist, yesterday and today, essentially
what it will be tomorrow or as St. Paul puts it, "until
Christ comes" (1 Cor 11:26), until the end of time.

B. HISTORICAL AND THEOLOGICAL NOTES

22.

THE CENACLE

The word Cenacle as applied to the site of the Last Supper comes from St. Jerome who in the Latin Vulgate has given **coenaculum** (dining room) as the translation for two different Greek words found in the Gospels and in the Acts **(anagaion** and **uperoon)**. The first **(anagaion)** found in Mark 14:15 and Luke 22:12, refers to the large furnished upper room designated by Jesus as the place where he would eat his last Passover and institute the Holy Eucharist. The average ancient Palestinian home was one-storied and flat-roofed. The homes of the wealthy, however, often included a guest room, penthouse fashion, on the second or upper floor, an outer stair often leading up to it. The word **uperoon** also means upper room and is applied by St. Luke (Ac 1:13) to the place where Mary and the Apostles stayed in prayer, presumably until Pentecost day.

By his translation St. Jerome suggests his opinion which identifies the two sites of the Last Supper and of Pentecost, an opinion which is shared by many recent commentators who point out that in the Septuagint the two words are used interchangeably.

Southwest of the actual walls of the Old City of Jerusalem, in the state of Israel, the memory of the Cenacle is attached to a large (45 by 29½ ft.) Gothic room of the 14th century on the second floor of an ancient building.

This is a rearrangement of an anterior chapel which was left dilapidated at the departure of the Franks. To the east of this room a stair leads to a bare chamber where the Moslems used to present a cenotaph (a simple plaster construction) of King David for the veneration of the Jews who formerly were not allowed on the first floor. This room is now empty and the Israeli venerate another cenotaph of David on the first floor. This is an interesting copy of a Roman sarcophagus but unfortunately it is hidden by a cheap wooden coffer covered with a carpet. Because of this shrine Mt. Sion has become a favorite pilgrimage spot for the Israeli.

The history of this site according to St. Epiphanius goes back to the first century of our era. This saint who died in 403 was a friend of St. Jerome and well acquainted with Judaea where he was born and lived for a long time before he became bishop in Cyprus. According to him the first Christian community had settled on the southwestern hill of Jerusalem and a little church which had been built there by the Apostles would have survived the destructions of Titus and Hadrian. In view of the remoteness of the site from the center of the Roman Aelia Capitolina this last remark is easily credible.

This important text of St. Epiphanius reads as follows: "Hadrian found the city in ruins except for a few houses and the little church of God built at the place where, after our Lord's Ascension of Mt. Olivet, the Apostles stayed in the upper room. In fact, it was there in the Sion quarter that the church had been built."

About 350 A.D., this old church was given needed restoration and in 390 a great basilica was erected near it, the church known in antiquity as Holy Sion. This basilica is clearly represented on the famous 6th century mosaic map at Madeba and was lovingly referred to by the Byzantines as "The Mother of All Churches."

Already in the 4th century and more generally in the

6th, this church was clearly identified as the site of the
Last Supper. Hesychius, a Jerusalem priest (c. 440) wrote:
"In thee (Bethlehem) flowed the virgin's milk, in Sion the
Holy Spirit descended from the bosom of the Father. You
baked the bread but Sion instituted the banquet; you
nourished the Savior in the manger but Sion led him
to the altar."

The Crusaders in 1099 when they captured Jerusalem,
found these two churches on Mt. Sion in ruins. They
restored the basilica in Romanesque style and with the
same dimensions, but of this construction nothing was
left after the destruction ordered by the Sultan of Damas-
cus, Melek-el-Moudahem, in 1219, 32 years after the cap-
ture of the city by Saladin.

The title of Holy Sion contributed to an erroneous
identification of the hill of the Cenacle with the Davidical
Sion which actually was on the opposite hill to the east,
Mt. Ophel, beyond the Tyropoeon valley. And so a tomb
of David appeared here in the 12th century and prompted
the Moslems' desire to possess the site.

The Franciscans in 1342 received in perpetuity from
Pope Clement VI the care of the Cenacle. It was then that
they built the small Gothic chapel described above and
which still stands today. The Moslems in 1523 transformed this chapel into a mosque and finally in 1551
expelled the Franciscans from the site. It is at that time
that the Friars founded their convent of the Holy Savior
in the interior of the city. The Father Custodian of the
Holy Land still prizes the title of "Guardian of Mt. Sion."

Today's Cenacle building cannot evidently be anything but a commemoration and an approximate localization, yet it clearly is deserving of reverence and respect.
The same, however, cannot be said for the later precarious detailed identification of the different rooms in the
building. There is evidently no reason to identify, e.g.,
the rooms on the ground floor, as where the lamb was

roasted, where it was eaten, where Christ appeared to
St. Thomas, where St. John said Mass, etc. Such un-
founded, unwarranted identifications should not, however, make us lose confidence in the credibility of the
basic souvenir of the institution of the Holy Eucharist.

Surrounding the modern tomb of David are various
chambers consecrated symbolically to certain important
events of Judaism in the past and in modern times.
Among others we might mention the chamber of the
Harp, a sort of Psalms museum; the chamber of the
Scrolls of the Law, containing ancient Bible manuscripts;
the chamber of Testimony with photos of the Old City;
the chamber of the Martyrs, dedicated to the millions of
Jews who were slaughtered by the Nazis.

The Franciscans were able to return to a new monastery **ad coenaculum** (near the Cenacle) on March 26, 1936,
but were obliged to evacuate during the troubles in 1948.
In 1960 they were allowed to reoccupy their monastery
and chapel which had been badly damaged by mortar
fire. The Israeli government has agreed to pay for the
repairs to the building.

Next to the Cenacle is the modern Church of the
Dormition which was built in 1910 on ground presented
by the Turkish Sultan to the German Emperor Wilhelm
II, who handed it over to the German Benedictines of
Beuron. This installation occupies part of the western
portion of the ancient basilica of Holy Sion.

For the first time, in 7th century, we find the specification of Mt. Sion as the site of Mary's Dormition. The
likelihood of the supposition was no doubt the reason
why it was immediately received with general favor and
why in the Middle Ages the Holy Sion basilica was graced
with the official title of "Sancta Maria de Monte Sion."

The erection in the valley of Josaphat, the upper Kid-
ron valley, of a Marian sanctuary designed to enclose
one of the tombs dug into the side of the Mt. of Olives,

dates back to the middle of the 4th century. The tomb had been venerated for some time as the place of our Lady's temporary burial.

23.

AN ANTIQUATED MINOR ORDER

A certain romantic aura attaches to the Roman catacombs, giving an entirely false picture of their nature and original use. They have been imagined as places of refuge and concealment for the first Christians in time of persecution. Consequently it was supposed that all the liturgy of the early Christian community was carried on underground in these cemeteries, and that not a few of the first Christians had even lived there. It has also been thought that all the Roman catacombs were connected with one another and with the churches within the walls. Even that they reached to Ostia, Albano, or Tivoli, or passed under the Tiber.

Actually, the catacombs were legally recognized and publicly accessible places of burial, and the phrase "The Church of the Catacombs" is a misleading, fanciful misnomer. No one could live in the mephitic air of the tombs, and few of the crypts or subterranean chambers were large enough to contain fifty people, whereas by the middle of the third century there were about forty thousand Christians in Rome.

The word catacombs derives from a Greek phrase which means "at the ravine." The Christian underground cemetery of St. Sebastian on the via Appia was originally known as "Coemeterium Catacumbas," because it is in a valley which gave the region its name, Catacumbas. Later the name catacombs was widely used for similar burial places, Christian or non-Christian, at Rome and elsewhere.

The most famous and extensive catacombs are those at Rome, but catacombs are not a Christian invention. Numerous catacombs are found elsewhere in Italy and in other places including Malta, North Africa, Egypt, and Palestine, and some northern European cities, like Paris and Trier.

Cremation, which was prompted mainly by economy of space, was the normal practice of pagan Rome in the first century A.D. The cinerary urns were placed in the niches of vaults constructed for this purpose and known as columbaria, so called because they looked like dovecotes. By the time of Hadrian (A.D. 117-138), however, cremation had given way to inhumation among the pagan population of Rome.

From the beginning, the Christians seem to have avoided the burning of the bodies of the deceased, and no trace of early Christian cremation has been found. Rather, the first Christians followed the practice of the Jews and Egyptians, and usually buried their dead underground, at Rome in the sepulchral chambers and galleries which are now known as catacombs. It should be noticed, however, that just as all catacombs are not necessarily Christian, so also all early Christian cemeteries at Rome are not underground.

The development of this specific way of burial at Rome was specially favored by the underlying geological formation. The city is surrounded by a great plain composed of materials of volcanic origin. There is sand and stone, and granular tufa, a soft stone composed of volcanic ashes and sand.

Abandoned sand pits **(arenariae)**, though they were already available, were not commonly used for burial because of the masonry involved. The porous tufa, on the other hand, is relatively easy to cut, and after it dries up, solidifies like stone. The Roman catacombs were usually dug in this kind of tufa or in soft limestone, the galleries sometimes branching off from a sand pit or a quarry.

The actual excavation was the work of a sort of workers' guild known as **fossores** or diggers. Their title appears in inscriptions on their own tombs, and they are depicted on the tomb slabs or wall paintings, holding pick, lamp, or spade, the tools of their trade.

The fossor was a skilled worker, something of a geologist and surveyor. He knew where to dig and respected property rights, keeping within a specified area and avoiding the undermining of highways. He was acquainted with water levels and forestalled possible inundations by digging well above the danger point. To him was also committed the preparation of the dead for burial as well as their internment. The inscriptions on the tombs and the decorative frescoes in the burial chambers were possibly also often their artifacts.

In a general way, the painters and sculptors who prepared the catacombal art work were not great artists, yet they expressed clearly the message they wanted to convey. The simplicity and graphic character of their work are a pleasant reflection of their faith and humble social condition and standing.

In the third century the fossores were counted among the clergy at the lowest grade. In St. Callistus, the official catacomb of the Church, they had a cubiculum (burial chamber) of their own; and from several inscriptions it appears that in the fourth century they had in their hands the management of the cemeteries under the control of the superior clergy. During the fifth century when the catacombs were no longer used for burial, the office of the fossores consequently disappeared.

The catacomb usually took the form of a network of interconnected corridors and chambers with burial niches

in the walls. Most of the tombs are in the corridors, the
chambers serving for more important people. The corridors are usually about three feet wide and a little over
six feet high. This corresponds roughly to a man's height
with a bit of additional room for the fossor to wield his
pick.

Most of the graves are simple rectangular box-shaped
horizontal recesses, known as **loculi** (compartments). The
corpses were laid, usually one to each loculus, and according to Jewish custom, wrapped in a winding sheet
and seldom embalmed. The opening of the loculus was
closed with two or three tiles or a marble slab. The length
of the body can be judged by the size of the grave.

Additional space was provided, when necessary, by
deepening the corridors. The floor of the gallery was dug
deeper to accommodate more graves, and sometimes this
process was continued until there were as many as a
dozen tiers of graves one below the other. Galleries were
often laid out in two, three, or more stories, the lowest
one being forty or fifty feet below the earth surface.

Today about thirty-five separate Christian catacombs
are known at Rome. It has been computed that the total
length of the catacomb corridors is between 60 and 90
miles, and that the number of tombs would be from
500,000 to 750,000.

It might be appropriate to include here some remarks
about Pope Damasus (366-384) who has been called the
poet of the martyrs. He did, in fact, give impetus to the
cult of the martyrs, because of his magnificent inscriptions in their honor.

There was hardly a cemetery at Rome which did not
have at least one of his inscriptions, and still others were
placed in the cemeterial basilicas and chapels. Most of
the original pieces have totally perished, many of them
probably at the hands of the Goths; but the text of about

forty of them has been preserved through copies made by pilgrims.

These inscriptions were composed in poetic style by Damasus and lettered by his secretary and artist, Furius Dionysius Filocalus. The text was carved on great white slabs of marble; the letters are majuscules, large capital letters, and painted red.

Damasus was not a great poet. His verses are not always regular, and he shows a lack of originality and versatility in his frequent repetitions of favorite words and phrases, many of them borrowed from Virgil. Yet his style was accounted elegant by Jerome, and he seems to have been a conscientious historian.

Pope Damasus placed one of his famous inscriptions on the tomb of St. Tarsicius in the catacombs of Callistus. This monument is of great importance because of its bearing on the dogma of the Eucharist. The story in the text is so unique and so different from the legendary motifs that we may confidently regard it as historical.

According to Damasus, St. Tarsicius was carrying "the sacrament of Christ." When the raging mob demanded that he show it to them, "he chose rather to yield up his life under their blows rather than to betray the heavenly members to the rabid hounds." In the first lines of the inscription, Damasus compares Tarsicius to the protomartyr Stephen, who also was slain by a tumultuous crowd.

The reference here is apparently to the ancient custom of sending to the titular (parochial) churches, as a sign of unity, some consecrated Eucharistic particles **(fermentum)** from the Papal Mass. The fermentum was to be used in the liturgy and was carried to its destination by acolytes who were grown men.

Later legend, which is perhaps nothing more than an elaboration of Damasus' inscription, has actually made

of Tarsicius a boy, and under this guise he has since become famous in Wiseman's Fabiola, as the saintly altar
boy, the martyred minor seminarian.

The inscription of Damasus shows plainly that the
early Christians believed in the real presence of Christ
in the Blessed Sacrament, and not only at the moment
of consecration or of communion. For them the heavenly
members of Christ were present at all times under the
consecrated species.

24.

MASS IN THE CATACOMBS?

A question of capital import for an understanding of early Christianity is whether or not, and if so, when and how, Mass was celebrated in the catacombs. It has too easily been imagined that all the liturgy of the early Christian community was carried on underground because of the constant persecutions. Actually, the facts show convincingly that for the first Christians, Eucharistic gatherings in the catacombs were more the exception than the rule.

During the first centuries, at Rome, the ordinary Eucharistic services were held within the city in private homes which were later known as the titular or parochial churches. The rites observed in the cemeteries were not the regular religious ceremonies of the community but a liturgical cult of the dead, or from the end of the third century, a memorial service for the martyrs, or possibly an occasional secret Mass during a time of persecution, as in the case of the martyrdom of Pope Xystus II. On August 6, 258, in Valerian's persecution, this pope was taken by surprise in the catacomb of Callistus and put to death with four of his deacons. The arrest took place as he was preaching, apparently as part of the celebration of the Eucharist.

In the fourth century, when the great cemeterial basilicas (St. Agnes, St. Lawrence, St. Sebastian) were erected above ground, the Holy Sacrifice was evidently the center of the liturgical functions there.

The fond opinion of former years that in the times of
persecution the regular liturgical services of the Roman
community were held in the subterranean cemeteries is
to be entirely rejected. Nowhere in the catacombs are
there rooms spacious enough for a fairly numerous con-
gregation. Moreover, there was no more security in the
cemeteries, but rather less. The cemeteries were known
to the police, so that a secret gathering could be much
more easily held in a private house. Incidentally, one of
the reasons the early Christians were at times called
atheists was that they had no regular temples or altars.

There is a definite probability, however, that the Eucharist was offered for the dead in the catacombs as it
was later in honor of the martyrs. At a very early date
the liturgy for the dead came into use, and was celebrated as closely as possible to the tomb of the deceased.
A careful study of ancient Christian funeral customs is
then necessary to penetrate to the roots of our question.

A curious pagan funeral custom, especially in the
cemeteries above ground, was the use of clay pipes leading down through the floor into the graves for the usual
libations of wine. A similar Christian custom was the
use of the **cataracta**, a hollow shaft inside an altar,
through which the faithful could lower small objects,
for the most part **brandea**, that is, small pieces of cloth,
to the tomb below. At St. Peter's tomb in the Vatican
plain hundreds of coins were obviously thrown in by
means of such a tube.

In the catacombs only a small fraction of the slabs
closing the graves carry any inscription. Small objects
such as coins, terra-cotta lamps, ivory figurines, bits of
colored porcelain, or pictures cut out of gold foil and
sealed between two pieces of glass **(fondi d'oro)**, were at
times pushed into the fresh mortar sealing the tomb.
Apparently these objects served as a means of identification; they also provided a modest decoration for the

grave. The lamps would serve a practical purpose as is clear from the traces of smoke that can still be seen.

Occasionally, though not very frequently, small flasks are found fixed in the mortar. These must have held liquid perfumes with which visitors would sprinkle the slabs closing the graves. The first archeologists interpreted these flasks or the broken bits of glass placed into the mortar as bottles in which had been preserved the blood of the martyrs. They are probably simply perfume receptacles and fragments of drinking glasses which had been used at funeral banquets.

The funeral agapes or love feasts were called **refrigeria** (refreshments) and originated partly in imitation of apostolic custom, partly in conformity with pagan usage. These meals were held by family groups who came to bury their dead or to remember them, or again at famous graves in remembrance of venerated saints, usually martyrs. The more numerous gatherings for the celebration of the funeral agapes were accommodated in buildings erected above ground, for example, the famous **triclia** (dining room) at St. Sebastian's.

This banqueting custom is evidenced archeologically by the funeral meal chambers, the **mensae**, the representations of meals, real or symbolic, and by grafitti mentioning a refrigerium promised by vow or accomplished, for example, in honor of the Apostles. Thus in the triclia at St. Sebastian a wall inscription states: "To Peter and Paul, I Tomius Coelius, made a refrigerium."

The **mensae** were stone tables set over or near a grave for the agapes. The Capella Graeca, in the catacomb of Priscilla, is a fine example of a funeral meal chamber. The chapel gets its name from two Greek inscriptions on one of its walls and dates back to the middle of the second century. The chapel is adorned with the most impressive series of early Christian paintings which is preserved in any single room of the catacombs. One of these paintings represents the raising of Lazarus. Christ appears in the center dressed in Roman style with a tunic and pallium, his left hand holding the garment. The right hand is uplifted in a gesture of speech. He is youthful and beardless with short hair and large eyes. Although it is now barely recognizable, this picture is of great interest since it is the oldest representation of Jesus that is preserved anywhere.

In another part of the cemetery of Priscilla, at the end of one of the quarry galleries, on the ceiling is a painting showing a mother, seated and holding her child, and with a star above her head. Standing beside her is a man dressed in a pallium and pointing upward with his right hand. This is probably a representation of Isaias prophesying the birth of Messias (Is 7:14) with the fulfillment of the prophecy indicated at the same time in the Madonna. The fresco dates back to about 200 A.D. and is the oldest known representation of the Blessed Virgin.

Along the sides of the Grecian Chapel runs a masonry bench with two simple graves underneath. Cushions and covers must have been spread around for the celebrations. The next chamber is a small kitchen with a cistern, waste-pipe, and fireplace.

The refrigeria were eventually discontinued, possibly because they tended to be roisterous, like the Corinthian agapes (1 Cor 11:21).

It is quite probable that the Eucharist could be part of the refrigerium. What is sure is that in the fourth century the papal crypt in Callistus was furnished with an altar and an episcopal chair.

Six chambers in Callistus, dating back to the third century and later, have been called the Sacrament chapels because of their fresco decorations. These chambers served not only as burial places, but probably also as tricliae. They were adorned with numerous paintings on the ceilings and on the walls between the graves. Several of these paintings represent banquet scenes.

25.

CHRIST AS ICHTHYS

In the art of the catacombs we have the first beginnings of Christian art before us. There is none earlier. Inscriptions, frescoes, and sarcophagal reliefs are the major types of art represented. There are also **fondi d'oro** (pictures cut out of gold foil and sealed between two pieces of glass) and terra-cotta lamps. The representations are simple yet graphic, and usually without backdrop or landscape.

Early Christian art did not hesitate to borrow from representations already familiar in pagan art (the dove, fish, ship, lyre, anchor, fruits, the seasons, Orpheus, the head of Medusa) using them in a decorative way or even giving some a Christian meaning. For example, the little winged Erotes or Amoretti on pagan tombs represented departed souls. But such signification had long since been forgotten and the little cupids were employed simply as decorations without offense to Christian taste, along with the butterflies, birds, and flowers. In the catacomb of Domitilla a fresco dating back to the first half of the second century shows a cupid holding a ribbon and a staff, instead of the usual bow and arrows.

The fish had already appeared in pagan art, but the Christians soon discovered that in the Greek language the five letters that spell fish form an acrostic, being the initial letters of the phrase, "Jesus Christ, Son of God, Savior."

Writing about 200 A.D. on baptism, Tertullian states:

"We little fishes, after the example of our fish, Jesus Christ, are born in water, and we cannot be saved if we depart from it." In the terms of this imagery the Church is some kind of aquarium.

Ambrose says that men are the fish caught by the fisherman, Peter, and that his hook does not kill but sanctifies. A very old inscription from the catacomb of Domitilla shows the cross as an anchor which has caught two little fish which represent the faithful. Augustine states that in the word fish "Christ is mystically understood because he is able to live, that is, to exist, without sin in the abyss of this mortality as in the depth of waters."

Thus the fish might stand symbolically for the name of Christ. In the catacomb of Priscilla there is an inscription reading, "Alexander in," after which a fish is shown, completing the phrase "in Christ."

Or fishes might stand for the Christians themselves. A grave inscription from around 200 A.D. has the word fish followed by "of the living" which must mean, "Jesus Christ, the Son of God, the Savior of the living." And it is adorned with two fishes which must represent the Christians who are the living.

The fish as a hieroglyph for Christ was also susceptible of varied application and remained a favorite theme of Christian iconography. St. Augustine's reference of the symbol to Christ's passion is interesting. Commenting on John 21:9, he remarks: **Piscis assus, Christus est passus,** the fish laid on the fire is the suffering Christ.

Christ as a fish was used in a special sense for Christ as food and thus for the Eucharist. The classical proof for this is the famous metrical inscription of Abercius.

In 1833, Dr. William Ramsay discovered in Asia Minor, two large fragments of this sepulchral inscription. In 1892 this was given by the Sultan to Pope Leo XIII and now adorns the Lateran Museum at Rome. With the help of

the epitaph of Alexander (a contemporary imitation)
and a Greek biography of Abercius, it is possible to restore the entire text of the inscription.

Abercius was a bishop of Hieropolis, a small town in
Phrygia. At the age of seventy-two he composed for his
own tomb, an epitaph in which he mentions his visit to
Rome and to such faraway places as Syria and Mesopo-
tamia. The date of the inscription is in the latter part
of the second century.

The text is written in a mystical and symbolic style,
according to the discipline of the secret **(disciplina arcani),**
to hide its Christian character from the uninitiated. This
metaphorical phraseology was the occasion for a sharp
controversy following the discovery of the monument.
Several scholars have believed that Abercius was not a
Christian but a devotee of the Phrygian goddess Cybele
or a syncretist. A closer study of the text, however, has
demonstrated beyond possible doubt that the content as
well as the language of the piece is Christian in character.

Here is a translation of this queen of all ancient Christian inscriptions. "I, the citizen of an eminent city, erected this tomb in my lifetime, that I might have here in
due time a resting-place for my body. Abercius by name,
I am a disciple of the holy shepherd who feeds his sheep
upon the hills and plains, whose eyes are large and all-
seeing, who taught me the faithful writings, and sent
me to Rome to see the royal city, and the queen robed
in gold and wearing golden shoes. There I saw a people
marked with the radiant seal. I also saw the plains of
Syria and all the cities, even Nisibis, beyond the Euphrates. Everywhere I found fellow believers, having
Paul as a companion, and everywhere faith led the way
and set before me for food the fish from the spring, the
pure fish of great size which the spotless virgin caught
and ever puts before the friends to eat. She has also
delicious wine and offers the mixed cup with the bread.

"I, Abercius, dictated this to be written in my presence, in my seventy-second year. Let every fellow believer who understands this, pray for Abercius. Let no one lay another in my grave under penalty of 2000 gold pieces to the Roman treasury and 1000 to my beloved native city, Hieropolis."

The theological importance of this text is evident. This is the oldest stone monument mentioning the Eucharist. The language of Abercius is poetic and somewhat enigmatic but he expects fellow Christians to understand his mystic symbolism.

This inscription probably illustrates the **disciplina arcani,** the fact that from the second to the fifth century, some care was exercised in certain quarters not to reveal to non-believers the Christian doctrine, especially relative to the sacraments of Baptism and of the Eucharist.

The holy shepherd of whom Abercius calls himself the disciple is Christ. The queen clad in gold must mean the Church in Rome, and the Christians are the people with the resplendent seal. The term seal for Baptism was well-known in the second century.

Abercius presents himself as a world traveler, having journeyed as far west as Rome, and east even beyond the Euphrates. Everywhere he found fellow believers, and everywhere substantial uniformity in ritual. He is acquainted with the Sacred Scriptures, and his reference to St. Paul is probably an expression of his predilection for the Pauline writings.

Christ is the big fish from the spring according to the well-known acrostic. The Incarnation is described rather phantastically as Mary's catch of the fish, and strangely enough she is the one who offers this food to the Christian friends. It could well be, however, that here the author's thought passes imperceptibly from Mary to the Church of which she is the prototype.

Christians everywhere partake of Christ in the observance of the Lord's Supper. The faithful receive bread as food and wine mixed with water, but faith tells them that it is really the great, pure fish, that is, Christ born of the Virgin Mary.

From the dogmatic viewpoint this inscription is of prime importance. Besides referring explicitly to the sacrament of Baptism and of the Eucharist, it supposes implicitly the divinity of Christ, the importance of the Roman Church, veneration for the Virgin Mary, and the communion of saints.

Another beautiful poem of the fourth century refers to Christ as the fish. It is known as the inscription of Pectorius and was found in an ancient Christian cemetery not far from Autun in southern France. The first five verses form the Greek acrostic ichthys.

"Divine race of the heavenly fish, draw with a pure heart, ye mortals, from the immortal fountain of divine water. Refresh your soul, my friend, with the perennial waters of wealth-giving wisdom. Take the honeysweet food of the Savior of the saints; eat with joy and desire, holding the fish in your hands. Lord and Savior, I pray, satiate us with the fish. I beseech you, light of the dead, may my mother rest in peace. Aschandius, my father, so dear to my heart, and my beloved mother and my brothers, in the peace of the fish, be mindful of Pectorius."

The references to Baptism and the Eucharist are again quite clear. Baptism appears as "the immortal fountain of divine waters," and "the perennial waters of wealth-giving wisdom." The Eucharist is described as "the honey-sweet food of the Savior of the saints." Christ in the first line is the heavenly fish, and again in the sixth and seventh stichs. The use of the term Savior three times is also meaningful. Finally, the ancient Christian ritual of receiving communion into the hands explains the words "holding the fish in your hands."

St. Cyril of Jerusalem, among others, describes this
ancient rite. The communicant received the body of
Christ in the palm of his right hand saying, Amen. He
was warned to be very careful not to lose any particle of
the sacred bread. He then partook of the consecrated cup,
bending low and saying again in the way of worship and
reverence, Amen.

The ancient stele of Licinia Amias, mentioned above,
is interpreted by some scholars as suggesting a Eucharistic meaning. The inscription starts with a wreath, then
on the second line is found "fish of the living." The next
space is pictorial: two open-mouthed fishes are rushing
from either side to an anchor. Only two more lines of the
original slab have survived. "To the worthy Licinia
Amias, she lived . . ."

The open-mouthed fishes are about to be caught by the
Christian anchor. Now in other representations the anchor is pictured as baited with the Christian fish, which
is called here the fish of the living, being considered as
the life or salvation of the living. The symbolism is a
bit complicated.

26.

EUCHARISTIC SYMBOLS IN THE CATACOMBS

One of the most ancient catacombal paintings symbolizing the Eucharist is found in the crypt of Lucina and dates back to the middle of the second century. It appears on a wall of a chamber and consists of two symmetrical representations of a fish, to the right and left of a lost central piece.

A basket full of small round loaves rests on each fish, or at least is so close in front just above the tail as to seem to rest on the fish. Inside the basket is a glass of wine which the artist depicted as showing through the mesh of the side. The configuration of a cup is clear enough and a red blur unmistakable as representing wine. If as seems quite probable the fish represents Christ, the intimate relation of the Eucharistic elements with the body of the Savior would be graphically illustrated. In any case, there can be no doubt about the fundamental Eucharistic signification of the whole, and of its Johannine (ch. 6) undertones.

Because there are two fishes facing each other, it has been thought that they represent the faithful who live in Christ and by Christ, and that the water under the fishes is symbolic of Christian baptism. This little problem could perhaps be clarified if the subject matter of the missing central panel were known.

Banquet scenes are frequently portrayed in the catacombs with fish and bread, and sometimes wine, as the components of the feast. It is not always certain, however,

whether these scenes depict the meals that were taken
in honor of the dead, or represent the Lord's Supper itself, or the heavenly banquet.

In the cemetery of Priscilla there is a fresco called the
Fractio Panis (breaking of the bread), a name given it by
Wilpert, its discoverer. It is found in the Capella Graeca
and is the oldest known representation of the Eucharist,
dating back before the middle of the second century.

Seven persons are gathered in a half circle **(sigma)**
around a slightly rounded table on which are placed a
plate with two fishes and another with five small round
loaves of bread. Seven bread baskets are ranged on either
side of the table, four to the left (as one looks) and three
to the right. The third guest from the right is a veiled
woman, her presence inculcating probably the universal
character of the gathering.

The person on the extreme left has his hands out-
stretched and somehow his feet are clearly seen above
the table. This is probably due to the artist's failure in
perspective, in his effort to make this character more con-
spicuous. In any case, a large cup with two handles is
before him and he is apparently breaking one of the
loaves, while the second, fourth, sixth, and seventh (left
to right) banqueters are attentive to his action. The third
and fifth (the woman) are looking the other way, possibly
simply for artistic variety.

This fresco may well be the oldest representation of
the Eucharistic rite. It is not absolutely sure, however,
that bread is really being broken, since that portion of
the painting is badly damaged.

Another probable portrayal of the sacrifice of the
Mass is found in the cemetery of St. Callistus in the
Sacrament Chapel A3, and is dated at the beginning of
the third century.

A man dressed as a sacred person and a philosopher

(with **pallium** and **tunica exomis**) stretches out his hands in benediction over a small three-footed table on which bread and fish are laid. The pallium is the Latin name for the Greek himation, a long shawl sometimes hard to distinguish from the toga, but much less voluminous. The exomis is sleeveless and short. Sacred persons were commonly depicted in a white pallium, and the exomis was characteristic of Greek philosophers.

To the right stands a woman **(orant)** with her hands uplifted in prayer, and symbolizing, no doubt, the Church.

The Eucharist most probably is portrayed here. It is not clear, however, whether the man is Christ or the priest in the act of consecrating. Yet it seems certain that the fish and bread are symbols of the Eucharist. It is also well known that in Christian antiquity the altar had normally the shape of a table, in fact, the altar was simply called a table **(mensa).** Even today mensa is the term used to designate the flat surface at the top of the altar.

A similar table with a fish and two loaves is found on the vault of a ceiling in Callistus. The loaves are marked with a cross. To the side of the table are seven baskets of bread. The date again is the end of the second or the beginning of the third century.

There are several examples of mystical meals in the chambers of the sacraments at St. Callistus. The figures are always seven; the baskets usually seven, but also eight or ten. Seven is simply the number of perfection according to ancient Biblical symbolism.

What dominates in most of the ancient banquet scenes is the Eucharistic signification. The idea of funeral agape, if present, remains in the background. At times, however, the stress seems rather on the heavenly banquet of the blessed, leaving implicit the Eucharistic symbolism.

The banquet as a symbol for heaven is a common

theme in the New Testament (Lk 13:29). This idea of the celestial banquet appears in later catacombal art, in the third century and the fourth.

For example, in a fourth century fresco in the catacomb of Peter and Marcellinus, four guests recline upon a semicircular sofa around a sigma table. Peace and love are personified as servants and everything points to the peace, abundance, and refreshment to be expected in the life to come. One of the guests says: "Peace, give me warm wine," another: "Love, mix me wine." Both are asking for the **calida,** a drink of wine mixed with warm water. Wine was commonly drunk warm, and always mixed with water because of the high alcoholic content necessary to keep the beverage for any length of time in bottles of skin or clay.

The sight of a shepherd carrying a sheep on his shoulders is familiar in the Middle East today, and representations of this subject are found not only in Greco-Roman times as, for example, in Hermes Criophorus (Ram-bearer), the protector of flocks who carries a ram on his shoulders, but also much more anciently. In Assyria and Syria, reliefs have been found from the eighth and tenth centuries B.C. which portray a man bearing a gazelle upon his shoulders, while the statue from Mari of a man carrying a kid in his arms is as early as the third millienium B.C. These older figures represent worshippers bringing animals for sacrifice, but at least by the time of the rambearing Hermes of Greece and perhaps much earlier the idea of the Good Shepherd was current.

In Christian art, the type was conceived anew and filled with Christian meaning. It appears much more frequently in the catacombs than any other symbol. Styger has counted 120 paintings and 180 plastic representations of this figure.

The Good Shepherd is now Christ himself (Jn 10:11) who carries the lost sheep back to the fold (Lk 15:5-6).

God in the Old Testament had also been presented as a
Shepherd (Is 40-11, Ez 34:12). The image of the Good
Shepherd is thus a Biblical illustration of God's Provi-
dence and of the redemption wrought by Christ.

The particular appropriateness of such a symbol in
Christian sepulchral art is plain enough. The shepherd in
the Old Testament Psalm 22 leads his sheep through
darkest gloom, a thought which is clearly most apt for
Christian burial.

It is interesting to note that the Good Shepherd is
the only theme in ancient Christian art which was often
presented as a statue. The early Church frowned upon
carving which was considered as easily leading to idolatry. But this shepherd idea was so plainly a symbol that
it was not very likely to be abused.

The famous statuette of the Good Shepherd, usually
dated in the third century and which is now in the
Lateran Museum in Rome, may have originally stood in
a cemeterial crypt. It shows the Shepherd as a beardless
youth, still in his teens, whose curly hair falls upon his
shoulders. He wears a tucked-up tunic and high stockings,
and has a basket slung on a strap. He carries the lost
sheep gently on his shoulders.

The Good Shepherd is usually surrounded by his flock
in the garden of his paradise. In the catacombs the presence of flowers and trees serves to indicate the celestial
paradise. A Christian would easily see here a symbol of
the peace of the redeemed, of those who live in Christ
even after death.

The juxtaposition of the orant and the Good Shepherd
is found as early as in the painting in the Lucina crypt,
where in alternating corners of a ceiling fresco are found
two shepherds and two orants. This combination recurs
frequently thereafter in Christian art, and its significance
is unmistakable. The Christian prayer for deliverance
in time of need and death is answered by the Good Shep-

herd who carries the soul safely home to its fatherland in paradise.

Later the Good Shepherd was depicted in the performance of the activities of his idyllic profession. In a third century fresco from Peter and Marcellinus, Jesus holds shepherd's pipes in his right hand. In a fresco from Callistus, the Good Shepherd carries a pail (mulcta) of milk symbolizing the Eucharist. In a crypt of Lucina, the pail of milk is placed on a small altar guarded by two sheep.

The Eucharistic symbolism of the milk is corroborated by the celestial visions of the martyr Perpetua (A.D. 202). The Good Shepherd appeared to the saint in a garden, surrounded by his flock. He was milking and gave her some curds, while those standing by said, Amen. In this vision of paradise she receives the proffered food as she received the Eucharist on earth according to the same rite, in the hands, while all those present say, Amen.

Ewes' and goats' milk was a staple food in Bible times, as it still is today in the Near East, and consequently the Christian writers of the third and fourth centuries saw in milk the element of flesh and blood.

After the fourth century, the figure of the Good Shepherd in Christian art seems to have been rapidly displaced by the Apocalyptic Lamb of St. John's Revelation.

Representations of a woman with arms uplifted in prayer, like that of the shepherd with a lamb on his shoulders, were also familiar in Hellenistic art. This figure recurs with great frequency in the Christian art of the catacombs but is invested with special significance. It is known as the orant and reflects the Hellenistic tendency to personify abstract ideas, a distinctive Christian figure, a personification of prayer for salvation and a symbol of Christian devotion. The early Christian writers explain the attitude of the orant as an imitation of

Christ on the Cross. The position was the Biblical posture
for prayer, especially of praise and thanksgiving.

Since the orants occasionally are shown in the garden
of paradise and have the name of the departed written
nearby, it is clear that they were also regarded as symbolic representations of the deceased. Some interpreters
have suggested that the soul of the deceased is thus portrayed as praying for the loved ones still on earth. It
seems more probable that the holy soul is represented
as giving thanks for its salvation, or even as still praying
for the ultimate redemption which includes the resurrection of the body.

In the Christian frescoes of the catacombs there is
little about Jesus' life story as such; only those features
which serve the special interests of the Christian community at that time were portrayed. Thus there is considerable interest in the two sacraments of Baptism and
the Eucharist.

Early Christian art avoided representing any of the
episodes of the Passion in a manner which would reveal
their stark reality. No painting in the catacombs of the
first centuries does so. Before the fifth century the cross
was rarely represented in catacombal art. It was usually
symbolized by an anchor, a lamb beneath an anchor, or a
dolphin over a trident.

27.

SAINT THOMAS AQUINAS

Soon after his death in 1274, St. Thomas Aquinas began to be known as the **Doctor Communis** because of the broad, quasi-universal character of his erudition, as manifested especially in his classical theological summa. The title **Doctor Angelicus** was first used in the fifteenth century. It is a tribute not only to the Saint's outstanding chastity but also to the speculative excellence of his elaborate treatise on the angels. In more recent times St. Thomas has been referred to as the poet and the theologian of the Eucharist (AAS, vol. 15, 1923, p. 320). On this particular point unfortunately, legend is intertwined, sometimes hopelessly, with historical fact.

The Saint did write his treatise on the Holy Eucharist at the end of his life, pouring into it the best of his acquired knowledge. We consequently have in this exposition a work of love, as it were, the great teacher's testament to his pupils, and already a sufficient reason for calling him the Doctor of the Eucharist. There are others.

Traditional Christian art often presents St. Thomas in a Eucharistic context, thus underlining the Saint's great devotion to the Blessed Sacrament. He is given special prominence in Raphael's great fresco, now preserved in the Vatican Museums, and often referred to as the **Disputa** or Disputation on the Holy Sacrament, a very inappropriate title. The artist really presents a hymn of glory in honor of the mystery of our Redemption. In the center of heaven, the upper portion of the

painting, Christ sits enthroned between his blessed
Mother and St. John the Baptist. His hands are out-
stretched so that his wounds are visible; the wound of
his sacred side is also apparent. God the Father dominates surrounded by angels. The Holy Spirit is at the foot
of Christ's throne between angels, two on each side,
holding the four books of the Gospels. Thrones on each
side of our Lord are occupied by two groups representing the elect in heaven. On the viewer's left are St. Peter,
Adam, St. John, David, and St. Lawrence; on the right,
St. Paul, Abraham, St. James, Moses, and St. Stephen.

The Holy Spirit in the form of a dove is coming to
earth and is the point of union between the two parts
of the picture. It is flying towards the altar which holds
the center of the lower portion of the painting, the terres-
trial zone. On the plain, unadorned altar table stands
a golden monstrance showing the Blessed Sacrament,
which is clearly meant as a focal point of the whole
composition. The altar is surrounded by doctors of the
Church, saints, popes, poets and artists, representatives
of the sciences and crafts. On the left among others,
St. Gregory, St. Jerome, Fra Angelico, Bramante; and
on the right St. Augustine, Innocent III, St. Bonaventure,
Sixtus IV, Dante, Savonarola. St. Thomas Aquinas is
near the altar, next to St. Ambrose. All are engaged in
meditation, adoration, or vocal praise of the Holy Sacrament.

St. Thomas is often represented with a radiant Host
on his breast, as a sign of his great love for the Blessed
Eucharist. Unfortunately legend has crept in with crude-
ly unrealistic details in a naive effort to illustrate the
fact. We are told, for example, that when St. Thomas had
extraordinary difficulties in his research, he would pray
before the Blessed Sacrament and even, in moments of
special fervor, open the tabernacle and insert his head
inside for special inspiration. This story is not found

in any of the ancient sources of the Saint's life and has
no intrinsic possibility. In those days there were as yet
no tabernacles on the altars. The Eucharist was usually
reserved in the so-called Eucharistic doves that were
suspended over the altar.

A fresco which adorns the Blessed Sacrament chapel
in the cathedral of Orvieto, represents St. Thomas in the
act of offering the Office of Corpus Christi to Pope Urban
IV. This brings up the question of St. Thomas' authorship
of the liturgical texts for the feast of Corpus Christi. The
problem is not without practical interest since parts of
the hymns for the feast are still used all over the world
whenever benediction is given with the Blessed Sacrament. The **O Salutaris, Panis Angelicus,** and **Tantum Ergo**
are hymns that are literally Catholic, that is, known by
Catholics all over the Church. And it is generally asserted
without further specification that St. Thomas Aquinas
is the author of the liturgical texts for the Mass and the
divine Office for the feast of the Blessed Sacrament. Recent research, however, has shown that such is not exactly the case.

No credence whatsoever can be given to the late, sen-
timental legend of the would-be contest between St. Bonaventure and St. Thomas Aquinas; the former would
have destroyed his manuscript after hearing the text prepared by his competitor. The story is found for the first
time in an anonymous work of the sixteenth century and
is apparently an adaptation of the fact that St. Thomas
prepared his glosses on the holy Gospels after St. Bonaventure had begged off for lack of sufficient time.

A Dominican legend has it that Pope Urban IV instituted the feast of Corpus Christi at St. Thomas' request
and as his recompense for preparing these commentaries,
his **Catena Aurea.** But the circumstances of the institution of the feast are well known and have nothing to do
with St. Thomas' Biblical work.

The legend of the crucifix at Orvieto from which St. Thomas would have heard our Lord saying to him, **Bene scripsisti de me,** referring to the Corpus Christi texts, is much later and has no traceable ancient literary source.

Actually the manuscript texts of the Office and Mass for the feast of Corpus Christi which have been preserved, reduce considerably the originality of the role of our Saint as author of this material.

St. Thomas had been asked by Pope Urban IV to prepare a liturgical text for the new feast, but for some reason that is not now too clear, another text was used for the first celebration of Corpus Christi. This text, the author of which is unknown, already contained the oremus, the hymns, and parts of the lessons of our actual Office, all of which St. Thomas retained in the text that he prepared.

There is also the added fact that St. Thomas' text has been considerably abridged and modified by the commission which under Pius V prepared the new edition (1569) of the breviary. Our actual text is none the less outstanding and truly worthy of its alleged author.

St. Thomas' main contribution is the arrangement of the Scripture texts. His antiphons are especially remarkable with a felicitous application of the different Psalms to the Blessed Eucharist. The response at Matins introduces a new device which, if it was not completely unknown before, at least had never been so well applied. They are presented as diptychs in which an Old Testament type of the Blessed Sacrament alternates with its New Testament realization in the Holy Eucharist.

Some scholars suspect that if certain parts of the preceding office were retained, it was not only because of their theological excellence but also because they might have had Pope Urban for author. This educated guess

cannot be proved historically yet it finds some confirmation in the fact that the Pope by natural disposition, as
witnessed in his Bull **Transiturus,** had a bent for lyricism.
On the other hand there is nothing in St. Thomas' tem-
perament or in his writings to denote any aptitude or
even taste for poetry.

Incidentally, the poetry of the hymns and of the sequence **Lauda Sion** is not quantitative as in classical
Latin prosody but accentual and rhymned as was the
custom in medieval pieces. Yet in spite of this technical
drawback the poems are still remarkable, especially because of their theological precision. One is inclined to
suspect that even if the Saint is not responsible for their
composition, he might have inspired some of the contents.

Although St. Thomas was not a musician, even the
music of the Office and of the Mass of Corpus Christi
has been attributed to him. The error of this reference,
however, is quite evident when the ancient musical
sources are consulted. All the music has been adapted
from earlier melodies, except that of the Introit and
Gradual of the Mass. And as the Saint was not musically
inclined, even these pieces should not be considered as
his compositions.

A last remark must be made relative to the readings
for the second nocturne of the office. Although St. Thomas
is apparently the author, the title **Sermo Sancti Thomae
Aquinatis** dates back only to the time of St. Pius V. And
the breviary reference to **Opusculum 57** is an indication
for the manuscript which contains St. Thomas' text for
the liturgy of Corpus Christi, not to his regular **Opuscula.**

Finally, the **Adoro Te** with its final verse **Pie Pelicane**
and **Jesu quem Velatum** are not part of the liturgy for
the feast of the Blessed Sacrament, yet are often thought
to have been written by St. Thomas. This hymn, like the
Ave Verum, forms part of the literature which originated

from the new ceremony of the elevation of the host after the consecration, in the twelfth century. Its author is unknown and the special meter and style suggest a different author than for the other hymns. The **Ave Verum** is attributed to Innocent VI (1352-62).

28.

EUCHARISTIC THEOLOGY TODAY I

The official teaching of our Catholic Church on the Eucharistic mystery has always been clearly stated. The Eucharist received much attention at the Council of Trent in the context of the Protestant Reformation. At the second Vatican the Blessed Sacrament again became a special focus of attention, this time, however, not so much because of prevailing controversy but because of its objective importance. The first document to be approved by the conciliar fathers was the Constitution on the Sacred Liturgy, Dec. 4, 1963, and since then there has been a constant proliferation of documents, showing the Church's solicitude and care for the Eucharist. About one third of the new edition of the conciliar and post-conciliar documents of Vatican Council II edited by Austin Flannery, O.P. (pp. 1-282, Liturgical Press, 1976) deals with this material and even there we have only a complementary selection of the documents which are not readily available. The Encyclical **"Mysterium Fidei"** (Sept. 3, 1965), for example, is not given, but among other important texts the following should be noted: the Instruction on the Worship of the Eucharistic Mystery, **Eucharisticum Mysterium** (May 25, 1967); the General Introduction to the Roman Missal, published as part of the Roman altar missal (March 26, 1970); and the Instruction on Holy Communion and the Worship of the Eucharistic Mystery Outside of Mass, **Eucharistiae Sacramentum** (June 21, 1973). The current Church-approved theology

of the Eucharist is then well specified and it does take
into account, at least initially, several current new approaches to the Eucharist which will be examined in
this study. It should be clear, however, that theological
investigation goes much further than these official texts
which are directed to the basic faith of the Christian
believer.

A recent phenomenon in the current history of the
theology of the Eucharist is the publication of many
agreed statements reached by Ecumenical groups on this
sacrament. Perhaps the most important was the "Windsor
Statement on Eucharistic Doctrine" issued on September
7, 1971 by the Anglican/Roman Catholic International
Commission which met at St. George's House, Windsor
Castle, England. These agreements, however, never had
any official status from the Churches involved and were
even the subject of serious contestation, and not only
from the Catholic side. The Catholic editors, Gerard
Butcher and Roger Nesbitt, published in 1973, **The Eucharist: Unity or Truth?**, Faith-Reyward Publications, Ilford,
Essex, pp. 138. This book consists of a series of essays
analyzing the Windsor Statement and questioning the
supposed agreement. As a sample of some Protestant
reaction to these agreed statements we might quote the
remarks of the Institute for Ecumenical Research, Strasbourg, France, on Lutheran-Roman Catholic Intercom-
munion. The research staff of the Strasbourg Institute:
G. Ansons, G. Gasman, M. Lienhard, H. Meyer, and V.
Vajta published an article in **Dialog** 12:224-230, summer
1973, entitled "Eucharistic Hospitality." According to
them among the Roman Catholic Eucharistic practices
"from which a Reformation understanding of the Eucharist must dissociate itself" (p. 227) before any real agreement can be reached are: the Roman Canon, private
Masses, and worship of the consecrated host. On such

conditions we will evidently travel different roads in-
definitely.

The Encyclical of Pope Paul VI, On Eucharistic Doctrine and Worship, **Mysterium Fidei**, received the expected rejection from some non-Catholic sources, but also
unwarranted criticism from a few Catholic theologians.
According to the "Lutheran View" of Vilmos Vajta,
Concilium 14: 157-166, 1966, the encyclical is based on
the sole initiative of the Pope and does not reflect the
leading theological trend of Catholic theology (p. 157).
Its doctrine is not the Biblically evidenced faith of the
universal Church. The Eucharistic cult of the reserved
sacrament advocated in the Encyclical is a great obstacle
to ecumenical unity (p. 166). According to the "Orthodox
View" of Metropolitan Emilianos Timiadis, **Concilium**
14: 167-176, 1966, neither the custom of private Masses
nor the devotion to the sacrament reserved in the tabernacle can be justified (p. 168). A Catholic editor found
the Encyclical distressing and confusing (**Commonweal**
83:42, 44, 1966). A Catholic theologian suggested that the
Encyclical missed the mark by not meeting today's theological problems (**Chicago Studies** 6:65, 1967). Such reactions seem self-destructive so that the mere mention
of them is implicit rejection.

Actually the Encyclical was issued in the wake of the
Constitution on the Sacred Liturgy, before the end of
the Council. It is a remedial document with the specific
purpose of correcting certain errors in speculative theology and in practice, errors current at that time and
still to be met nowadays. For example, the insistence that
the sign value of the Eucharist is the total and exhaustive
explanation of the real presence of Christ in the Eucharist; or again teaching and practice based on the notion
that Christ is no longer present in the consecrated host
after the celebration of Mass (no. 11). Unlike the Consti-

tution on the Liturgy, the Encyclical is not a comprehensive document of renewal of the Church's Liturgy; its purpose is rather to subserve the Liturgy Constitution by safeguarding dogmatic truth and presenting the basic elements of Eucharistic theology. The Pope demands the active participation of the faithful in the Eucharistic celebration and points to the reception of Holy Communion as the highest form of liturgical participation (no. 31). Yet he insists that the whole reality of the Eucharist must not be syphoned from the altar into the assembly, into the presence of Christ by his word, or into his presence by faith in our hearts (nos. 35-38). As a reaction to the current downgrading of devotional Eucharistic practices, the Pope points to the permanent presence of Christ in the Eucharist as a focal point for personal devotion but only as closely linked to the spirit of the Eucharistic celebration (no. 66).

The Instruction **Eucharisticum Mysterium** like the Encyclical MF is pastorally oriented. It insists on recentering all aspects of the Eucharist around the community celebration of the Eucharist as a memorial of Christ's death and resurrection. It stresses the revaluation of the word of God in the liturgical celebration where word and sacrament should be understood as a single act of worship. It suggests that the only possibility of survival for Eucharistic devotions lies in their integration with the Eucharistic liturgical celebration of the Mass. As in the Constitution on the Liturgy (no. 7) the different modes of Christ's presence to his Church in the liturgical celebrations are highlighted (EM, no. 9). This is perhaps the principal and basic theological orientation of Vatican II.

The general Instruction which prefaces the new Sacramentary (1970) gives an excellent summary of the actual Eucharistic faith as practiced in our post-Vatican II Church. The New Roman Missal puts in better perspec-

tive within a wider framework of doctrine and practice
the traditional faith of the Church in the sacrificial character of the Mass, in the real presence of Christ under the
Eucharistic species (without prejudice to his other real
presences in the liturgical celebration) and faith in the
unique role of the ministerial priest. A special feature of
the new order of the Mass is found in the periods of social silence (cf. Ernest Lussier, **Living the Eucharistic
Mystery**, 1976, p. 81-86, "The Theology of the New Sacramentary").

The current theological thought on the Eucharist is
very active and productive: witness the constant flow of
books and of articles in the different periodicals. In a
survey, which I have been conducting as a hobby since
1968, I have noted the publication of 328 recent books,
and I have annotated 1746 articles; and the survey is re-
stricted to French and English material. There are a certain number of topics that surface from this study and I
should like to present them here for a brief examination.

First, the Church-accepted explanation of the Eucharistic mystery by the concept of transubstantiation is
being discussed, even contested, in view of a new approach styled as transignification and transfinalization.
Then the real presence of Christ in the Eucharist is now
better explained as a personal presence in the context of
Christ's many different ways of being present to his
Church. The central nature of the Mass in the Christian
economy is now stressed and the mystery of the Eucharistic sacrifice is better understood by reference to the
Paschal mystery and the eternal priesthood of Christ.
The social character of the Eucharist and the ethical approach to the sacrament are also being considered, as also
the communitarian nature of Christian worship. Much
is also being written on the renewal of Eucharistic devotions.

Other subjects about which there is much literature,

but which will not be treated here are the following. The most frequent topics now are the Liturgy for young Christians and the Ecumenical Agreements, inter-communion and Eucharistic hospitality. There are also many articles about the Liturgy in small groups, home Masses, folk Masses, and Masses for the handicapped; about the Eucharistic prayer (the Canon of the Mass) in general, and about the new Eucharistic prayers; about concelebration and celebration style; about first Communion and confession before Holy Communion; about Sunday Mass and music in the Liturgy; about the history of the Mass and liturgical theology; about Eucharistic spirituality; about the role of the Holy Spirit in the Eucharistic celebration; about the Eucharist and the resurrection of Christ, the Eucharist and the sacrament of the dying; about the evangelizing power of the Eucharist, the ministerial priesthood, the general priesthood of the people of God, and the possible ordination of women; about the implications of liturgical prayer for personal meditation and contemplation; about the prayer crisis and the Eucharist; about Eucharistic celebrations in the charismatic movement and healing through the Eucharist; about the Eucharist and holy Scripture. The field is as vast as it is timely and interesting.

Today sacramental theology is taking new directions in its approach to the sacraments in general and the Eucharist in particular. In addition to the problems mentioned above in relation to **Mysterium Fidei,** new difficulties are constantly cropping up. One often finds a depreciation or even a total elimination of the notion of sacrifice, so that the Eucharistic celebration is degraded to being simply a friendly meal and the tabernacle a mere pantry for the care of the sick. Some are suggesting that the sacraments are antiquated, that they no longer mean anything to the people of our time, or at least that they are too far removed from a person's daily life. Consequently the word of God in the liturgy is sometimes being replaced by some secular readings which are judged more appropriate; some even attempt an invalid replacement of the Eucharistic bread and wine. There is also the problem of the so-called underground liturgies where people put in practice their avant-garde theories which are propagated by word of mouth but are considered too advanced to be put into writing because of a backward, step-dragging Church. A case in point is that of the nun who quit her campus post after being charged with saying the Mass (**National Catholic Reporter,** April 26, 1974, p. 3).

Recently some have become very sensitive to everything that is human and pertains to man, but it is not clear why this should in any way affect what is God's and transcendent. In sacramental matter much importance is given to the evaluation of the sign and the actual signifying, but the signified, the essential, is often glossed over: for example, in the Eucharist the sanctifying presence of the Risen Lord. The research is directed to bringing out the truth of the sign, but less to the invisible realities of faith. Thus in the Eucharist both in the catechesis and the liturgical practice, the deep content of the dogma is often practically evacuated. To define the Mass as a celebration or a sharing of the word and of the bread is a minimalist description which brings to mind a fraternal agape rather than Christ's Last Supper, a ritual meal of the highest importance, and the sacrifice of the cross which is reproduced in an unbloody fashion in the sacrifice of the Mass. Twenty centuries have taught us to treat these tremendous mysteries with respect and reverence. We should not, under pretext of renewal and authenticity, allow them to be reduced to the level of a simple human exchange. If, for example, the liturgical vestments, the sacred vessels, the ritualistic decorum are no longer there, with the sacramental signs, we run the risk

of eroding the mystery itself. The love of God has to be
the foundation, the life, the motivation of our brotherly
love. A Eucharist without the gift of Christ's Paschal
presence is an empty human ceremony.

And now after the recent liturgical reform some are
asking not **how** to celebrate the sacraments but **why**. Do
faith, hope and love really need sacraments? Is the acceptance of Christian rites really a criterion of Christian
identity? Is it not just as right before God to be an anonymous Christian? Agonizing questions that find their answer in a theology of the Church which would establish
the proper balance between the Church as an event, as
the people of God, and the Church as an institution.

Faced with such a situation could it be that theology
is completely detracted and impotent? There are three
main directions which current theology has taken in its
process of renewal: a return to Biblical and Patristic
sources; a better understanding of sacramental symbolism; and the reintegration of sacramental theology into
the theology of the Church, Ecclesiology. And it must be
pointed out immediately that in all this, especially in the
study of symbolics, in itself a difficult science still in its
infancy, much work remains to be done.

Contemporary theological research has abandoned
much of what appears decadent in Scholasticism. In particular, Dom O. Casel, O.S.B., with his mystery approach
to the sacraments, especially the Eucharist, has sent
Christian theology back to the world where our Liturgy
originated and developed, and from which it cannot be
separated. For Casel the Eucharist contains the actuality
of the historical act of salvation, not as a repetition of
history but on the transcendent level.

The modern approach to the study of symbolism (e.g.,
in P. Tillich and Karl Rahner, **Theological Investigations**,
vol. 9, pp. 9-49) has contributed its share to the renewal
of sacramental theology and at the same time a crop of

new problems. Symbolism is an essential part of all sacraments. It should not in any way be identified with the imaginary or seen as opposed to what is real. **Eucharisticum Mysterium** has stressed the theology of the sign, the meaning of the different elements found in the Eucharistic celebration, a first step on a new and difficult road.

Perhaps the most fruitful approach to the sacraments and to the Eucharist in particular is by way of ecclesiology, by situating the Eucharist as the center of the life of the Church considered as the great sacrament of Christ, who himself is the sacrament of our encounter with God. One will recognize here the title of E. Schillebeeckx's book.

With this general summary, or status quaestionis, as a background our next chapter will focus on four points of Eucharistic doctrine as seen in recent theology: transubstantiation; Christ's presence in the Eucharist as a personal presence; the central nature of the Eucharistic celebration as the Paschal mystery; and the social, communitarian nature of Christian worship and the ethical approach to the sacrament.

29.

EUCHARISTIC THEOLOGY TODAY II

After the overview of current Eucharistic theology as presented in the first part of this study, we can now focus our attention on four important points of Eucharistic doctrine: transubstantiation; Christ's presence in the Eucharist as a personal presence; the central nature of the Eucharistic celebration as the Paschal mystery; and the social communitarian nature of Christian worship and the ethical approach to the Sacrament. These are evidently highlights in the Catholic theology of the Eucharist and nothing more is attempted here than a practical summary approach. The presentation is made in a pastoral style, avoiding as much as possible strictly technical language, while attempting to state as accurately as possible current thought.

Especially since the Council of Trent, the Church has presented the term transubstantiation as an apt formulation for the Eucharistic mystery: "Christ is made present in this sacrament by the change of the whole substance of the bread into his body and of the whole substance of the wine into his blood; this unique and truly wonderful change the Catholic Church rightly calls transubstantiation" (MF, no. 46). This statement of the encyclical is a quotation from the Council of Trent. The subject matter of the dogma taught at Trent is the real presence of Christ in the Eucharist which is not only a spiritual encounter but also an incarnational extension of the Paschal mystery. The Council did not canonize

any system of philosophy but attempted to state in apt
words what the Church always believed: "It has always
been the conviction of the Church and the holy council
now again declares" (Denz-Schon, nos. 877, 884).

Many today are not satisfied with the explanation of
the Eucharistic real presence by the idea of transubstantiation which they see as a medieval Scholastic thesis
which does not really clarify the mystery but rather
creates new difficulties. They no longer accept the view
that there is a reality upholding the world of phenomena,
and conceive matter as an agglomeration of atoms, elec-
trons, neutrons and protons. Our popular language no
longer understands the terms substance and accidents in
the Scholastic meaning of the words. These theologians
do not question the Eucharistic mystery but seek a new
formulation in the terms transignification and transfinalization. The consecrated bread and wine receive a new
finality and signification which goes beyond their ordinary signification and finality. The meaning and purpose
of things vary according to circumstances. A ring may
be just a piece of metal, a personal decoration, or a pledge
of deep love and devotion. A piece of ordinary cloth is
really and objectively changed when it becomes my country's flag. The change that takes place in the Eucharist
is due to Christ's effective intention; the bread and wine
are identified with the gift of his body and blood. The
Eucharistic meal is an effective sign of Christ's real gift
of himself. The presence of Christ imagined as transubstantiation risks an exaggeration of local presence, as of
a thing contained in the tabernacle. Transignification in
the language of existential phenomenology stresses the
relation of the being considered not in itself or for itself,
but for others. The Eucharistic presence is not meant
for itself but for others. It is a real presence of Christ in
the host but it is meant to promote God's presence in our

hearts. What is stressed is less the mode of the real presence but its purpose, less the how than the why: our personal encounter with our Lord.

Not everyone, however, is ready to give up the notion of transubstantiation: witness Father Paul-Laurent Carle's (O.P.) book, **Consubstantiel et Transubstantiation** 1974, Imprimerie Taffard, Bordeaux, pp. 104; and the recent article by Charles Cardinal Journet in **The Thomist**, 1974, pp. 734-746. Here is the gist of the Cardinal's argumentation. There does exist a most mysterious way that permits a being, without undergoing the shadow of a change, to be present in a most profound manner where he had not been previously. It is primarily thus that God makes himself present in his creation, the Word in the Incarnation, and the Holy Spirit in our justification. God creates by an act of his omnipotence, without the slightest ripple appearing in the ocean of the divine being. God has, as it were, summoned the world to himself, breathed it forth out of nothingness. The Word begins to exist outside the Father, without changing, in a human nature, by drawing this human nature to himself, by assuming it. In justification the Holy Spirit transforms the heart of man but the change occurs only in man. These three presences are thoroughly real but in each the change is uniquely that of things to God and not inversely. So also in the Eucharist, Christ becomes wholly present here below without change of his being but with the sole, utterly profound change into him of bread and wine. In the Eucharist as in the Incarnation, bodily presence and personal presence cannot be separated. There are not two Christs, but two modes of presence of the one Christ: one natural in the glory of heaven, the other sacramental under the veil of the externals or empirical activities of bread and wine. The bodily presence of the Savior in those who receive communion lasts but the space of time during which the sacramental species are still unaltered. But such visits are like flashes of fire or bolts of lightning.

Other theologians point out that the Eucharist is a transcendent mystery whose only apodictic credibility lies in faith based on the authority of God's revelation, precisely, Christ's institution at the Last Supper. It could be that transubstantiation goes further than is warranted by our modern theories on physical matter, and that transignification does not explain enough by not going further than the signs of bread and wine; and in any case there is no possibility of any totally convincing explanation of the Eucharistic mystery really going further than the visible sign of the sacrament and the omnipotent word of our Lord.

That there is just one presence of Christ to his Church, manifested in different ways, all of them real presences, and with the Eucharistic presence as the presence par excellence, is now a commonplace (SC, no. 7; MF, nos. 35-38; EM, no. 9) that need not be labored here. The Eucharistic presence, nevertheless, has always posed difficult theological problems, and today, perhaps more than ever, this presence seems difficult to many. Eucharistic piety has tended to stress one's personal encounter with Christ, as a tête-à-tête, an intimate communion with our Lord. The liturgical renewal, on the other hand, has concentrated on Mass as a community celebration, and somehow a tendency has developed not to see in the Eucharist the presence of someone but an action, a means, a holy and sanctifying thing, and above all, a meal of Christian fraternity, so that the tabernacle, for all practical purposes, becomes simply the larder for the sick members of the community. This evidently is a misconception of the personal presence of Christ in the Eucharist.

Earthly realities can never give the total explanation of any Christian mystery. It is eschatological and can only be understood in the light of the Paschal mystery; our risen Lord is the only full and total explanation of the Christian message. So also the key of the Eucharistic mystery is not in the signs of bread and wine, nor in the community meal understood either according to a philosophy of nature or of intention; the risen Christ is the only sufficient explanation of the Eucharistic mystery. The Eucharist is intelligible only as the presence of the Paschal Christ who comes to his earthly Church. The presence of the risen Christ is the foundation of all the other dimensions of the Eucharist, as it was the essential of the faith and experience of the original, the first Christian community. And it is a **personal** presence worked by the power wherewith Christ submits all things to himself (Ph 3:21).

Personal presence is more than a mere relation in the contiguity of time and space; it is better than temporal or local presence. Personal presence seems to be the mode of presence which is normative for the interpretation of the Eucharist. It should be noted first that the personal presence of Christ in the Eucharist is not merely spiritual, for the person of Christ is embodied and includes a physical presence. This word **physical** used in MF, no. 46 has been criticized, but without reason. The adjective means belonging to reality, and is used in the sense of bodily, pertaining to the body, the risen body of Christ. Christ's presence is not a dream or a mere memory; Christ is present in all his Paschal reality. The consecrated bread and wine become for us in all reality our ark of the covenant, our tabernacle, our temple, the particular meeting place where having met Christ, we can go out and perceive him, recognize him in a thousand other places as well: in others, in events, in everyday life, in my conscience, my heart, in the Bible and especially in the Gospel, and in the other sacraments.

Christ himself, who is never absent from us, but present in all kinds of ways, who indeed can never be otherwise among us than as totally present as the imagination can conceive (though of course not necessarily perceived to be so), renders himself objectively accessible to us in the Eucharist, both in his compassionate grace and in the drastic summons to discipleship. Christ is really not **on** the table but **at** the table with us; he is our Host, we are his guests. In the Eucharist Christ is really there for us in a reciprocal relationship; **communication** is essential to personal presence. Christ's Eucharistic presence is an invitation to personal communion, a personal gift of himself. It enhances our own personhood and makes possible and perfects our presence to one another.

This understanding of Christ's Eucharistic presence as his personal, Paschal presence, as the presence of our risen Lord, clarifies our understanding of the sacrifice of the Mass. The Council of Trent laid much stress on the relation of the Mass to the sacrifice of the cross, and had very little to say about the glory of Christ's resurrection which is an essential part of the Paschal mystery. Vatican II has remedied this situation: "The Church has never failed to celebrate the Paschal mystery, the Eucharist in which the victory and triumph of his death are again made present" (SC, nos. 6, 47 etc.). The risen Christ is the Paschal Christ, eternal in the death in which he was glorified, living forever the mystery of our redemption which has two faces, his death and his glorification. The Eucharist is a sacrifice precisely because of the presence of our Paschal Lamb. One is a Christian by communion in Christ's death and resurrection, and the Mass is the official way of doing so.

This is where Casel's idea of the Eucharistic celebration as the actualization of the Paschal mystery appears in full accord with the Biblical revelation on Christ's eternal priesthood, which is the continuation of his earthly priesthood. Paul sees Christ "there at God's right

hand pleading for us" (Rm 8:34). He ascribes to the glorified Christ an activity that continues the objective aspect
of our redemption. Christ presents to the Father his obedience, his sufferings, his prayers and our prayers, our
worship sanctified through him. "He is living forever to
intercede for us" (Hb 7:25). He lives forever functioning
as Mediator and Priest, on behalf of his people; his intercession is not an offering, which has been made once and
for all, but a continual representation on the ground of
the completed offering. As it was for man's salvation
that Christ lived on earth, so also it is for the same purpose that he still and ever lives in heaven. John has the
same description of the Paschal mystery when he sees
"a Lamb with the marks of his slaughter upon him" (Rv
5:6). This indicates the perpetuity of Christ's priesthood,
the continuance of his mediatorial office. By his sacrifice
Christ won his victory, and in the Eucharist, because of
the personal presence of the Paschal Lamb, the risen
Christ, all succeeding generations have his sacrifice ready
at their disposal.

A last question to be treated briefly is the social character of the Eucharist, the ecclesial and communitarian
nature of Christian worship, and the ethical approach to
the sacrament. This last point again is consonant with
the constant teaching of the Bible which already in the
Old Testament (Am 5:21-27) rejects any divorce between
worship and practical living. It is a fact that the practical,
lived dimension of the Eucharist is not sufficiently ac-
knowledged. There is still too much triumphalism in Eucharistic worship, especially in paraliturgical devotions.
We are still also too ritualistic and legalistic in our men-
tality, and individualistic in our piety, while neglecting
the very meaning and purpose of the Eucharist, which
is the unity and growth of Christ's mystical body, the
Church.

One of the main pastoral concerns of Vatican II was

the participation of the faithful in the liturgical celebrations, a solicitude which is found also in all the literature that we have been examining. This thinking is closely related to the pastoral approach to the Paschal mystery and to the theology of the Church. Some theologians see the sacraments as signifying and effecting in our spiritual life something similar to the growth and progress found in our natural life. Others consider them as remedies to the seven capital sins. St. Thomas saw them as gravitating around the Eucharist as a focal center. A recent favorite approach stresses the ecclesial approach to the sacraments: Baptism, Confirmation, and Holy Orders make the Church; the Eucharist gives it growth and unity, Marriage perennity; Penance and the Anointing of the Sick offer remedial help. But no matter how the sacraments are seen we are always led to the same evident conclusion: they are meant for us men and demand our full co-operation. One quotation from Vatican II should suffice: "Mother Church earnestly desires that all the faithful be led to that full, conscious, and active participation in liturgical celebrations which is demanded by the very nature of the liturgy. Such participation by the Christian people as a chosen race, a royal priesthood, a holy nation, a purchased people (1 P 2:9) is their right and duty by reason of their baptism" (SC, no. 14). We must graduate from a theology of "confection" in which the principal concern is the proper performance of the ritual, to a theology of celebration in which the emphasis is rather on the quality of participation. And this extends beyond the liturgical action itself to include the whole faith-life of the Christian community.

A final word should be said about Eucharistic devotions which unfortunately are so neglected since Vatican II. This neglect is surely contrary to the mind of the Council and the clear directives of the post-conciliar documents, especially EM and ES. The principle laid down by SC is clear and convincing: "Popular devotions of the Christian people are warmly commended, provided they accord with the laws and norms of the Church. These devotions should be so drawn up that they harmonize with the liturgical seasons, and accord with the sacred liturgy, are in some fashion derived from it and lead the people to it, since the liturgy by its very nature far surpasses any of them" (SC, no. 13). This centering of the official life and devotion of the Church on the sacred liturgy is one of the great principles of Vatican II theology.

To be theologically authentic, Eucharistic devotion must approach the presence of Christ in the Eucharist as a personal sacramental presence, as a sacrificial and communal presence. Eucharistic devotion must be the Mass held in meditation; it must exploit the mystical dimension of the Eucharist, reflect the highlights of the Eucharistic celebration, especially its aspect as memorial, praise, and communion; bring out its eschatological character and emphasize the principal effect of the sacrament which is the unity of the Church.

Finally, here are a few books dealing with the new theology of the Eucharist. **New Approaches to the Eucharist** by C. O'Neill, O.P., Alba House, 1967, pp. 126. **Eucharistic Theology,** by J. M. Powers, S.J., Herder and Herder, 1967, pp. 192. **His Presence in the World: A Study of Eucharistic Worship and Theology,** by Nicholas Lash, 1968, Pflaum Press, pp. 214. **Theology of the Eucharist** by James Quinn, Fides, 1973, pp. 94. **Getting to Know the Eucharist,** by Ernest Lussier, SSS., Alba House, 1974, pp. 190. **Living the Eucharistic Mystery,** by Ernest Lussier, SSS, Alba House, 1976, pp. 208. **The Mass: An Historical, Theological and Pastoral Survey,** by Josef A. Jungmann, S.J., Liturgical Press, 1976, pp. 312. **Theological Dimensions of the Liturgy** by Dom Cyprian Vagaggini, O.S.B., Liturgical Press, 1976, pp. 952.